CALIFORNIA ASSET PROTECTION GUIDE

(The NON-Legalese California Business Owner's & Professional's Guide to Asset Protection & Tax Planning)

Reed K. Scott, MBA, JD, LL.M. (Tax)

Reed K. Scott
E-mail: reed@yesllp.com
Website: www.yesllp.com

Limits of Liability and Disclaimer of Warranty
The author and publisher shall not be liable for your misuse of this material. This book is strictly for informational and educational purposes.

Warning – Disclaimer
The purpose of this book is to educate and entertain. The author and/or publisher do not guarantee that anyone following these techniques, suggestions, tips, ideas, or strategies will have a successful outcome. The author and/or publisher shall have neither liability nor responsibility to anyone with respect to any loss or damage caused, or alleged to be caused, directly or indirectly by the information contained in this book.

For access to more insights on asset protection, wealth planning, tax savings strategies, business planning, and more, go to www.yesllp.com and register for our free weekly e-mail newsletter and blog.

"Business owners have a problem: unlimited exposure to bogus lawsuits. Expert lawyer Reed Scott delivers the goods and sheds light on a little known strategy that is the future of asset protection: the Private Retirement Plan^{SM}."

James Cunningham Jr., Esq, Certified Specialist –
Estate Planning, Trust & Probate Law, CunninghamLegal

"As a California business owner, I've been trusting the author to protect my business for years. If you have anything worth protecting from a lawsuit in California this is THE book you need to read!"

George Barberick, CEO, D&D Lift, Inc.

"The author has taken the legalese out of asset protection and translated it into plain English. It's a no nonsense book for the California business owner, and should be required reading for CPAs practicing in California."

Phil Wilson, Tax Partner, Marcum LLP

"As a financial advisor to California businesses, the first thing I focus on as we're building for retirement is protecting assets. Reed understands California asset protection like no one else. I recommend him to all my business clients."

Kelly F. Crane, CFP®, CFA, CLU
President & Chief Investment Officer Napa Valley Wealth Management

My heartfelt appreciation to my clients, who have trusted me to help them protect their assets, build their businesses, their wealth, and their dreams, and to my parents, Leslie and Marie Scott, for giving me love and discipline in equal measure.

About the Author

Reed Scott is an attorney, who in addition to his law degree, has an MBA in finance and a master's in tax law. He has been a financial analyst for Ford Motor Corporation, and corporate counsel and president for a technology consulting company based in San Francisco. He is managing partner at Youngman Ericsson Scott, LLP, a respected law firm in in Northern California with over 9,000 clients. The firm focuses on asset protection, tax, and wealth planning and provides a full range of services to business owners and families.

Reed was originally drawn to asset protection planning because he saw a member of his own family and many of his clients spend years and often decades trying to accumulate wealth and avoid taxes only to lose everything due to unexpected circumstances and things that seemed outside of their control. After much research and experience he began to develop techniques for protecting families and businesses from the unexpected. Reed began showing people that what seems outside of our control doesn't have to be. Unfortunately, the marketplace for asset protection is confusing and often full of conflicting advice. Business owners, doctors, and other professionals get conflicting advice from their advisors, much of it not only wrong, but dangerous. Often, elaborate asset protection schemes are put in place that accomplish nothing, and sometimes even worst - the business owner is so confused they do nothing. Asset protection planning is, in his opinion, full of schemers who are more than willing to take advantage of the confusion to sell elaborate plans that business owners or professionals won't know is worthless until it is too late.

Reed is also a sought-after speaker who gives dynamic seminars on wealth planning and asset protection, and has educated thousands of business owners, professionals, and consumers on asset protection techniques and tax minimization strategies.

FREE E-BOOK!
"RETIREMENT ACCOUNT RICHES"

Learn how to turn a modest retirement account into a multimillion dollar family dynasty!

"Retirement Account Riches" is a book that shows you how to make sure your retirement accounts can minimize taxes and maximize value!

Most Americans don't realize the power the tax code gives them to create wealth. Quit complaining about taxes and use them to your advantage! This book details just how to do that.

Learn how to avoid the critical mistakes people make in their retirement accounts. Make sure you download your **FREE** copy today from **www.yesllp.com.**

Table of Contents

"Left to themselves, if something can go wrong it will."
~ The First Corollary of Murphy's Law

Introduction
Why Protect?

W hy is asset protection needed? Incredibly, smart people still ask me this. They say things like, "It seems like an unnecessary expense... won't my insurance cover this?" These are likely people who have never been sued before, or have little to no experience with the United States Judicial system.

If you have been sued as a business owner or professional you would know that insurance companies have exclusions and many reasons why they won't pay your claim, and as I'll relate later from my own personal experience, sometimes they just state you aren't covered when you both know you are. Their position is often, "if you think we're wrong then sue us and prove it!"

Even if your insurance does pay, the judgement may exceed the amount of your insurance. The financial damages for loss of life of a child on your rental property or in a car accident could well exceed the amount of your policy.

Then there is always the professional or business person just starting out who tells me: "I don't have anything yet, so what can they get?" How about a judgement hanging over your head to attach future assets and/or a percentage of your income for the rest of your life? Does that sound like an attractive prospect?

It's surprising that often otherwise intelligent people want to play Russian Roulette with everything they've worked for their entire lives, but this is still the case.

This book isn't written for them. It's for the thousands of successful California business owners and professionals who work hard, do the right thing, create jobs, and help people, and as a result amass wealth. It's for smart people that know better than to leave everything they've worked for at risk. If that's you read on.

Why I Do What I Do

I dropped out of the University of Kentucky Law School to work in a family business when I was 22 (I finished law school later, but yes, I was a law school dropout). The business was successful and owned by my oldest brother. He was 14 years older than me and had a very successful career in business. He had two very profitable and successful multi-million-dollar heavy truck dealerships in Michigan.

Business was growing, he was opening new dealerships, and the plan was to sell them to me after I learned the business in few years. He wanted to diversify into other businesses.

This prospect sounded much better to me than spending years in law school and then struggling to try and build a law practice, that even if successful wouldn't pay me anywhere near the money I could make from my brother's truck business.

Everything kept going great for a couple of years, and then the unexpected happened (this is usually the way when it comes to asset protection – it's never what or when you think it will be). The trucking industry was deregulated, and industry sales went from approximately 500,000 new trucks sold per year to about 150,000. A third or so of the dealers in Michigan went out of business. My brother didn't go out of business right away; it happened over a period of years as the industry never bounced back and sales remained low. During those years as he fought to survive he went deeper and deeper into debt. Eventually he lost everything. His business, his home, his cars, his motorhome, his cash, and almost his family. The emotional toll was devastating, and due to privacy concerns I am not going to share the emotional impact these events had on him, his wife and his children.

I was young, I was not yet an owner of the business, and I had no liability so there was nothing to lose but my time and my youth. I did learn a valuable lesson: never work hard to acquire something you don't have a plan for keeping.

There's a great movie starring Robert DeNiro called *Ronin*. In the movie DeNiro plays an undercover CIA agent trying to track down the possible sale of a nuclear device. In one of the opening scenes of the movie, DeNiro has to meet someone he doesn't know in a bar, but before he goes into the bar he goes around the back, makes sure the exit door is unlocked, and then plants a gun where he can retrieve it if needed. Once his contact checks out (Jean Reno) and they are leaving the bar, DeNiro retrieves the gun he had hidden. Jean Reno asks him did he always hide guns around bars and DeNiro replies: "I never go into a place I don't know how to get out."

Good advice, and equally applicable to asset protection. Never own an asset without protecting it. When people ask me "Do I need to do asset protection planning?" I answer, "Only for the assets you'd like to keep."

I wrote this book to cut through the confusing world of legalese and provide practical solutions to hard working business owners and professionals. Many asset protection attorneys speak in legal jargon that is confusing, or they are trying to sell you a one size fits all solution they have a vested interest in (like Nevada Attorneys selling Nevada LLCs). In addition, if you talk to three different attorneys you will often get three different recommendations on how to best protect yourself. Not only that, but most attorneys have never run a business other than their law firm. They went from undergraduate school to law school. Maybe they spent a few years working for another company, but most have never dealt with the complexities of handling employees, selling, managing a business, or as a doctor perhaps having someone's very life in your hands.

I have been in business and I know how frustrating it is to deal with attorneys who don't understand business and don't speak the language of business owners or non-attorney professionals. If I have a gift, it is for translating complex subjects into language everyone can understand.

This book will explain your various asset protection options in plain simple English. I have no vested interest in selling you a particular solution as I am not even your attorney. Therefore, hopefully you will take this information in the spirit with which it is intended - to prevent you from having to go through the devastating nightmare that my own brother and his family went through. (Good news though, he is now more successful than ever and every asset he owns is fully protected).

If you haven't figured it out by now, let me make it clear for the hundreds of lawyers who will read this book and say: "Oh yeah, but what about this, or what about that?" This is not designed to be a book for lawyers. It is not an exhaustive legal treatise of asset protection techniques. This is a book for people who are tired of hearing "it depends" answers. It's for those who want straight forward solutions to implement now, without all the equivocations that lawyers normally give. Clients ask me: "What would you do?" That is what you will find out in this book and these are my opinions. (If you are an attorney looking for more detail or an exhaustive treatise on asset protection techniques not just for California, but globally, I highly recommend: *Asset Protection Strategies and Forms* by Dustin I. Nichols, Mark A. Ziebold, and Alan Eber.)

The California Environment: The Perfect Storm

Why did I choose to write a book limited to California business owners and professionals? Why not expand my opportunity and sell to the entire United States?

For one, there are already plenty of attorneys who do that, and in doing so they don't necessarily speak to the uniqueness of the largest market in the United States - California. In my opinion, by trying to cover everyone, they do California a disservice. As you'll see later in this book, asset protection is very jurisdictionally driven, and what you can do in one state won't necessarily work in another. What your friend can do with their business in Texas and Nevada may or may not work in California. Additionally, believe it or not, California has some unique asset protection opportunities that are not available in other states, and they are not covered in other books possibly because there is little opportunity for attorneys and financial advisors to make money suggesting them as they are so easy and straight forward to implement.

California is unique not just because of its size, but also because of the legal environment. California is the most litigious state in the Union according to the National Federation of Independent Business

(NFIB). In fact, NFIB has ranked California as the #1 "Judicial Hell Hole" for the last three (3) years (2013-2016).

The judges and courts in California give very little respect to elaborate asset protection schemes to protect debtors. To say California is a creditor friendly state would be the epitome of understatement.

I do not want my clients to have to explain to a California judge why we are using a Nevada LLC when my client has no relationship to Nevada. They don't live there, they don't own a home there, they don't even have a bank account there. Yet there are well respected attorneys writing in national publications that this is the solution for a California business owner, and you can go on the internet and set one up in a day.

I have had clients move out of California to take advantage of asset protection laws in other states. That is certainly one option, but the good news is it isn't necessary. In fact, California has some options that are only available to California business owners.

In fact, I recently met with a very successful business owner and went through all the available protections available in other states. At first, he said he was ready to move. Then, when I went through his California options, he said "Why would I leave and give that up?" Let's go through your options and see if you feel the same way!

Definitions

This book is not designed to include technical jargon on asset protection planning. You will see it is very conversational and full of examples. However, just to make sure everyone is on the same page I am going to briefly define a few basic terms.

1. **Exemption**: A legal right under federal or state law to have certain assets unavailable to creditors under any circumstances. Not an asset transfer, therefore cannot be fraudulent or voidable. For example, a state homeowner's exemption, the funding of your 401(k) plan, or the funding of a California retirement plan.

2. **Irrevocable Trust**: A trust that cannot be easily changed. Often used for asset protection and tax planning.

3. **IAPT - International Asset Protection Trust or Off Shore Trust:** An irrevocable trust set up under the laws of a non-United States jurisdiction such as the Cook Islands or Belize. A jurisdiction that does not respect United States judgments.

4. **DAPT - Domestic Asset Protection Trust**: An irrevocable trust set up in a state where the legislature has enacted special laws, allowing for a trust to provide asset protection features. For example, Delaware, Wyoming, Nevada, Alaska, South Dakota, Ohio, etc.

5. **LLP - Limited Liability Partnership**: A form of ownership where all the owners receive limited liability. In California this type of entity is only available to professionals such as doctors, lawyers, and architects and does not shield them from malpractice liability, only general liability such as someone getting injured on the premises or the liability of a partner.

6. **LP - Limited Partnership**: A partnership with two classes of partners - general partners and limited partners. The general partner has unlimited liability and is responsible for running the partnership. The limited partners have limited liability if they are not running the partnership. The general partner is usually shielded by a separate entity such as a corporation, LLC, or irrevocable management trust.

7. **LLC - Limited Liability Company**: An entity designed to give the members limited liability from acts of the company and from acts of the individual members. Like a limited partnership, but does not require a general partner to provide protection to the members. Every state has their own version, i.e. Nevada, Wyoming, Delaware, California, Alaska, etc., and some states grant differing levels of asset protection. Can be taxed as either a partnership, an s-corporation, or a disregarded entity (meaning it will be treated as a sole proprietorship on your 1040).

8. **FLP - Family Limited Partnership**: Same as a limited partnership, except the limited partners are all family members and the operating agreement should be drafted to keep membership in the family upon divorce, bankruptcy, lawsuits, etc.

9. **FLLC - Family Limited Liability Company**: Same concept as an FLP, except using an LLC arrangement that has a family oriented operating agreement. This eliminates the need for a general partner.

10. **Fraudulent Transfer Act**: Law stating that a transfer of an asset for less than full value in an effort to hinder a creditor is fraudulent, and therefore such transfer can be undone. The creditor must prove the transfer is fraudulent by "clear and convincing evidence." A higher standard than the new California Voidable Transfer Act.

11. **Voidable Transfer Act**: Effective January 1, 2016, this law states that a transfer of an asset for less than full value in an effort to hinder a creditor is not valid, and therefore such transfer can be undone. The creditor has only to prove the transfer is voidable by a "preponderance of the evidence." A much easier standard for California creditors.

12. **ERISA - Employee Retirement Income Security Act**: Federal law enacted to protect the retirement assets of Americans. ERISA plans are an example of assets protected under a federal exemption.

13. **Qualified Plans**: Retirement plans that meet the requirements of ERISA

14. **Non-Qualified Plans**: Retirement plans that are not qualified under ERISA but are still valid for tax planning purposes, such as an annuity.

15. **Federal Exemptions**: Laws that protect your assets under federal law, for example qualified retirement plans.

16. **State Exemptions**: Laws that protect your assets under state law, for example the homestead exemption, or a California retirement trust under California Civil Code 704.115.

17. **California Retirement Plan**: A retirement plan created by the California legislature in 1970 (see above) to protect the retirement assets of union employees and business owners in California.

18. **Exemption Planning**: An analysis done to make sure you are using all your federal and state exemptions that should be a part of any asset protection planning.

19. **Tax Exemption Planning**: An analysis of your tax returns and business operations to ensure you are taking all your available federal, state, and local tax credits and exemptions, both personally and for your business.

20. **TPA – Third-Party Administrator**: A company specializing in setting up and administering your retirement plans.

Section I
Asset Protection vs.
Exemption Planning

3

"Property must be secure or liberty cannot exist."
~ *John Adams*

Chapter 1
Your Maybes vs. Your Rights

T he Declaration of Independence says we have certain "inalienable rights" like the right to life, liberty and the pursuit of happiness. In the quote above, John Adams even stated that secure property is a requirement of liberty.

And yet, in California, a creditor can take your home, your bank accounts, a portion of your future earnings and maybe any future assets you might be fortunate enough to accumulate. It doesn't matter to your creditor's lawyer that you, your spouse, and your children might need a place to live. It can all go away in an instant.

Who are the potential creditors of a business in California? You name it, they are a potential creditor. Some business owners think creditors are someone they owe money, but think again. For example, a creditor could be employees claiming you didn't enforce their required breaks under state law. They call the California labor board and after an investigation the board finds you guilty, not only on one count, but for all your employees going back years. The state awards treble damages to every employee amounting to hundreds of thousands of dollars each. Millions in judgement forces your business into bankruptcy. Those employees who you sweated for and sacrificed for to make sure they had a job are now your creditors. Believe it or not, I have even heard of law firms hiring investigators who get themselves hired as employees, so they can investigate from the inside and educate your employees of the amount of money they can get by filing a claim. Despicable? Yes. Do you think this is covered by your liability insurance? Ask your insurance agent. You violated the law, insurance doesn't like to pay claims that are a direct result of your unlawful acts.

Perhaps you manage an employee stock ownership plan and your plan doesn't do that well. Can your employees sue you for mismanagement of their plan? The answer is yes.

What if one of your employees kills someone while driving a company vehicle? The person they kill is a 25-year-old professional with a lifetime earning potential of $10,000,000. The judgement against you is $10,000,000. Your insurance pays $5,000,000 (because you have a larger policy than most), that leaves you with $5,000,000 to be taken out of your pocket. If there aren't assets inside the corporation to pay the debt, the attorney will try and pierce the corporate veil and go after you personally. If you think it's hard to pierce the corporate veil you should talk to a litigator. They are going to subpoena all your corporate records and if you didn't cross every t and dot every i, then say goodbye to your personal assets, such as your house.

But wait! Where are your property rights as stated under the Declaration of Independence? Didn't John Adams say secure property is a prerequisite for liberty?

John Adams didn't live in California, and he didn't live in a time where attorneys are willing to do anything to make a buck. The system is a game and they know how to play it. They don't create anything of value for society, but they sure can destroy the value you built. Remember, I'm an attorney talking. I've seen the system in action and it is broken. Don't depend upon the judicial system to protect you - avoid it at all costs. How can you do this? To start, claim your inalienable rights under the law: your legal federal and state *exemptions*.

What is an Exemption?

An exemption is a right that you have under the law. You are entitled to it as a citizen of the United States if it is a federal exemption, or as a citizen of the state you live in if it is a state exemption. If you claim it no attorney or creditor can take it from you. But, and this is a big but, you must CLAIM it. There are certain things you must do to claim your right and each right is different. For example, under federal law you can contribute money to a retirement plan, such as a 401(k), IRA or defined benefit plan if available. Federal ERISA Law

(Employee Retirement Income Security Act) states if you do this, the money you have contributed is absolutely protected from creditors (there are some limitations on IRAs, but I will talk about this later).

So, if you have contributed to a 401(k) savings plan and over the years and you have accumulated $1,000,000 in the plan (or any amount, there is no limit to the amount protected in a 401(k) or qualified plan), this amount is absolutely protected under federal law and no state law can trump it.

A good example of this is the O.J. Simpson case. You may remember that O.J. Simpson was acquitted of the murder of his ex-wife and Ronald Goldman. What you may not remember is that the Goldman family sued O.J. in civil court and won a wrongful death claim. As a result of that judgement they took everything O.J. owned, including his Heisman trophy! Well… not quite everything. What they didn't take, because it was protected under federal law, was O.J.'s NFL Player's Union Pension Plan Account. This was protected under federal law, just like your 401(k) is protected.

Even though the wrongful death judgement was not fully satisfied by O.J.'s other assets, the Goldmans still could not touch his NFL Player's Union Pension because it was exempt.

O.J did not have to set up an elaborate asset protection plan to protect his pension. It was automatically protected just like your 401(k) plan is *automatically protected* or *exempt*. You don't have to transfer the asset. You don't need to hide the asset. It is already set up the way it needs to be protected the moment you contribute.

This is an example of a federal exemption, but do states have exemptions? Some do, some don't; each state is different. To give you an example of a state exemption let's go back to O.J. for a moment. You may remember that after the murder trial, O.J. was often shown coming out of his Florida mansion on his way to the golf course, where he was surrounded by reporters. How is this possible? How could he have a Florida mansion when he still owed money to the Goldman Family for his wrongful death judgment? The answer is Florida has a *homestead exemption*. In Florida, your home, regardless of its value, is absolutely protected from creditors as long as it is contained within one quarter (1/4th) acre. Additionally, except for bankruptcy cases, Florida has no statutory time period for which you need to wait before you are eligible for this protection. In other words, if you kill someone, and can buy a home in Florida while the trial is going on, your home is protected. Even if you lose the civil wrongful death claim, Florida will NOT allow a creditor to take your home (the exception for the waiting period is bankruptcy - you must be a resident of Florida for four years to have your home protected from a bankruptcy judgement).

So you see, O.J. had no asset protection planning and he was able to claim his "rights" under federal and state law. His retirement was protected under federal exemption law, and his home was protected by exemption under Florida state law.

By the way, is there anything that can negate or take away your right? Yes - ignorance. Ignorance can negate most things. For example, if you try to set up and administer your own 401(k) plan at your company. You attempt to calculate the amount each employee can contribute, you do the tax reporting, and you mess up; in that case you have negated your right. If you try to set up your own trust in Florida without an attorney, and you transfer your home to it without applying the homestead exemption, you have lost your right. You may call this being frugal, I call it being ignorant. Whatever you call it, same result.

Most intelligent business people hire a third-party administrator to set up and manage their retirement plan, and if they follow the rules your right will stay in place. Most smart Floridians will not try to set up their own trust, or transfer their home into it and hence will keep their right. This is true with most rights. They will protect you from everything except ignorance.

Rights vs. Maybes

Now we've discussed exemptions, whether state or federal, as your rights in property. Absolute rights that protect your property from creditors. So, what's a maybe then?

A maybe is anything else that you use to try and protect your property. Yes, anything else. This is what most attorneys call "asset protection planning". When most people, including attorneys, talk about asset protection planning, they are talking about "transferring ownership" of an asset from one form of ownership to another, in the hopes of you being able to keep that asset in the event of litigation or financial setback.

For example, when an attorney creates a limited partnership (LP) or limited liability company (LLC) to protect your investment real estate, they then record a new deed showing the ownership of the real estate is now the LP or LLC. If they don't transfer the real estate into the LP or LLC, you won't get the protection of the entity. This is called an "asset transfer".

What is the protection of the LP or LLC? As the title implies, the protection is "limited," not absolute, like an exemption. For example, if you hold your real estate investments inside an LLC, and a child dies in a fire on one of your rental properties, the judgement from a lawsuit against you might be $10,000,000. Let's say that your rental property inside the LLC is worth $1,000,000. As the incident occurred on a property "inside" the LLC, the court could award the entire $1,000,000 property to the people who won the judgement (the child's family). Your assets outside the LLC, however, are protected from the lawsuit. This is called "inside liability." Your assets outside, not owned by the LLC, would not be available to this creditor because you isolated them from the assets inside the LLC. This is called "outside liability."

The reverse could also be true. You could have a rental property inside an LLC, and have a child die in the swimming pool at your personal residence (not owned by the LLC). If the child's family won a $10,000,000 judgement against you they could take your home, your bank account, your brokerage account, and perhaps garnish your wages up to 25% of your income until the judgement is paid, but they could not get the rental property inside the LLC because the incident happened outside of it, and the rental property was isolated against the "outside liability."

As you can see most asset protection planning is "limited." Also, there is no guarantee a court will uphold the protection of an LLC or LP. In California, courts have dissolved LLCs in lawsuits, exposing the assets to judgement creditors. This has happened with LLCs formed in other states as well, as I will detail in Chapter Five. Because asset protection is limited and in some cases, there is none at all, I call these "maybes" as opposed to the "rights" you have under exemption planning. This is why exemption planning is so much more powerful than asset protection planning.

If exemption planning is more effective than asset protection planning, why don't more attorneys offer exemption planning? Why can you Google "asset protection attorneys" and get several pages of results, then search "exemption planning attorneys" and get very few results? Even the results that come up for exemption planning won't necessarily be for the right kind of exemption planning. Most attorneys that come up when you Google exemption planning are estate planning attorneys, and they work on exempting estates from estate tax, which has nothing to do with what we're talking about (protecting your assets from lawsuits).

In my opinion, the reason attorneys aren't offering exemption planning is simple - they can't make money with it. I could make much more money selling clients elaborate entity structures like corporations, family limited partnerships, out-of-state LLCs, domestic asset protection trusts, and offshore trusts in the Cook Islands or Belize than I can by simply showing you how to take advantage of your exemption rights under federal and state law.

Why am I telling you about exemption planning in California then, if I can't make money at it? The same reason I don't sue people for what I believe are cases that shouldn't even be in the court system. I feel it's the right thing to do.

Don't get me wrong. I set up all kinds of entities for clients. I set up corporations, asset protection trusts, LLCs and LPs just like other attorneys, but part of my planning includes telling clients what their exemption rights are in California, and making sure they get them before anything else. Often, if a client picks up all their exemptions, it reduces the need for more elaborate and complex planning. My smartest and wealthiest clients often do three things. They have insurance, they pick up all their exemptions they are entitled to, and they set up some asset protection entities. This type of layered protection, in my opinion, is the absolute best you can have, and is worth every penny. After all, you didn't work all your life so you could turn over your life's savings to someone trying to get rich off of your innocent mistakes. Yet this is what happens every day in California, perhaps the most litigious and business unfriendly state in the nation.

I believe it is irresponsible to set up elaborate protection entities for clients without also advising them to pick up their rights under exemption law. If my clients should decide, after I tell them what their exemption rights are, that they don't need the additional layer of planning, and I lose money because of it, then so be it. My rule is the old adage "do unto others as you would like them to do unto you," and I don't know about you, but I would sure rather have a right than a maybe!

"Comparison is the Death of Joy."
~ Mark Twain

Chapter 2
California vs. Other States Exemption Rights

Many of my business clients complain about California. They compare themselves to businesses in other states, not only in terms of tax rates, but also in terms of state exemptions to protect property.

I can understand this. As I mentioned in the previous chapter, states like Texas and Florida have some attractive exemptions under state law compared to other states. For example, in Texas and Florida, your home has unlimited protection regardless of its value. This is called the state "homestead exemption." In California we have a homestead exemption too, but it is a lot lower. In California, a creditor can take your home in a lawsuit, but the homestead exemption allows you to keep $75,000 of the equity if you are single and $100,000 if you are married (California Code of Civil Procedure §704.710).

This is why you see all the multi-million-dollar mansions on the beaches in Florida. Wealthy executives, business owners, and professionals from other states have built homes there and are ready to make it their primary residence in the event of a successful lawsuit. Except for bankruptcy, there is no waiting period. In other words, when the business owner in Michigan loses a lawsuit he can move to his house in Florida and doesn't have to prove he was a resident for any period of time before the judgment. He just lives there. (For bankruptcy he must have been a resident for four years prior to have the state homestead protection).

Pretty incredible difference, right? You can lose your home in one state and be absolutely protected in another just because of a difference in exemptions. It hardly seems fair and yet unfortunately, I have been practicing law for many years, and fairness is rarely a successful argument.

So, what do I tell my California clients? Do I tell them to move to Texas or Florida? No, because in California we have some powerful exemptions as well, it's just that they aren't quite as common knowledge as the famous Florida and Texas homestead exemptions. After all, O.J. moved to Florida to live in a mansion, and he had the news media following him around everywhere he went. However, as I'll illustrate in the chart below, with proper planning a California resident doesn't have to leave the state for powerful exemptions.

I don't have room in this book to compare California exemptions to every state, but below and on the next page is a chart comparing California to three of the states known for personal exemptions that protect your assets: Texas, Florida, and Nevada. For a state by state comparison you can go to www.legalconsumer.com for a more complete comparison between states.

Exemption	Texas	Nevada	Florida	California
Homestead	Unlimited	$550k	Unlimited	$75k single or $100k married
401(k)	Unlimited	Unlimited	Unlimited	Unlimited
IRA	Unlimited	Unlimited	Unlimited	Limited to extent reasonably necessary for support CCCP§ 704.115
Life Insurance	Unlimited	Cash value attributable to premiums not to exceed $15,000 per year in premiums	Unlimited	$12,860

Exemption	Texas	Nevada	Florida	California
Annuities	Unlimited	$350/month	Unlimited	$12,860
Wages	100% Exempt (except for child support)	75% Exempt	100% up to $750 per week and 100% of disposable earnings* for someone earning above $750 per week Fla, Stat. Ann. 222.11	75% Exempt
State Private Retirement Plan	N/A	N/A	N/A	Unlimited CCCP§704.115

* *"Disposable earnings" means that part of the earnings of any head of family remaining after the deduction from those earnings of any amounts required by law to be withheld.*

As you can see, all the states have California beat significantly in every category, except one. None of the other states have a state exemption for a private retirement plan. This is an exemption exclusive to California and was passed by the California Legislature in 1970. The federal retirement law ERISA was modeled after it and has been around and tested in court for many years (I have listed the more prominent court cases in the appendix). I will go into more detail about the private retirement plan in Chapter Five, but for now know that it is the one unique state exemption that makes California an attractive state for a business owner. Yes, can you believe it? Despite the horrible business climate for taxes and litigation, there is actually something that may convince a successful business not to move out of state! If you're a Californian considering retiring to Nevada, for example, to avoid the high California income tax, you should note from the above chart that Nevada only protects equity in your home up to $550,000. On the other hand, with a properly drafted and maintained California private retirement plan you could protect all of the equity in your home, and your real estate investments as well. By protect, I mean exempt, not the limited kind of protection you get under a charging order with a

Nevada LLC! Remember, with an LLC, no matter what state it is formed in, a creditor can tie up your property with a charging order. With exempt property, the creditor gets nothing and can't tie up your property! I don't know about you, but I would rather have a creditor get nothing.

Ok, now you're saying, "I'll move to Texas or Florida then, because my home will be 100% exempt." But what about your investment real estate? What about your stocks and bonds in a brokerage account? Are they exempt in Texas or Florida? Absolutely not! You are back to the same problem as Nevada. The best you can do is an LLC or limited partnership, and any creditor can tie up your property and sit there like a vulture waiting for you to sell or distribute profits. Eventually you will have to distribute profits because you need to pay the taxes on the income you earned, and that is when the creditor pounces. California is the only state with an exempt private retirement plan. Why only protect your home? After all, you can't retire with just your home, you need other assets protected, and that is why the California Legislature created the private retirement plan. Don't leave it on the table just because no one is selling it to you. No one sells you your homestead exemption either, because there is no way for an advisor to make money on it, but does that mean you shouldn't take it?

Section II
The Three Biggest Mistakes
in Asset Protection

"Put all your eggs in one basket...the handle's going to break. Then all you've got is scrambled eggs."
~ Nora Roberts

Chapter 3
Umbrella Insurance

I speak about asset protection throughout the state of California. Groups and organizations invite me to speak about a topic important to their members, protecting their hard-earned assets from lawsuits and creditors. People must think I'm at least somewhat knowledgeable on the subject since they keep inviting me back. And yet, there is always someone in the crowd who tells me they have umbrella liability insurance, and after listening to me maybe they'll get more, but that's all they need to do.

Prospects come into my office, often referred by one of my existing clients. They'll ask me what they need to do to protect themselves, then they go away and do nothing because what I told them required some planning and expense, and they wanted to "think about it." I sometimes find out later from the referrer that they got more umbrella liability insurance, even though I advised that that was not sufficient.

Let me give you an example of why depending on umbrella insurance may be the biggest and last business mistake you'll ever make. A construction company in California had 100 employees. The owner of this corporation had a large umbrella insurance policy (ten million dollars). He had been a successful and profitable company for over 25 years and some of his employees had been with him that long. One day, he got a notice from the California Department of Labor that he was in violation of the Labor Code for not providing adequate breaks for his employees. Not only was he in violation for the current year, but he had been in violation for many years, according to the Department of Labor.

How did the Department of Labor come to this conclusion? Many of the company's long-term employees filed complaints against him for not giving them breaks. Was it true? According to the business owner, he had given strict instructions to his construction site foremen to make sure the workers got their breaks. According to the foremen (the ones who were still at the company), the workers often refused their breaks because they wanted to complete the job. This wasn't going to cut it with the Department of Labor; they needed evidence and records of employee education, and there wasn't any.

The owner found out that a relatively new employee had told his colleagues that they were eligible for a large personal lump sum cash reward against their employer for violation of their rights (with treble damages under the Code, some awards per employee exceeded hundreds of thousands of dollars). This "new employee" turned out to be an investigator for a law firm who specialized in Department of Labor Code violations and helping employees get the maximum award.

Does this sound unjust to you? It does to me, and yet that company depended on their umbrella insurance to protect them. Guess what the insurance company said when the company owner filed a claim to protect his business and his personal assets? "You broke the law and your policy excludes claims resulting from breaking of criminal or administrative rules. In addition, there are punitive damages, and your policy specifically excludes punitive damages." Game over – the company went broke and filed for bankruptcy protection.

Or how about the investor with $15,000,000 worth of real estate held in his own name. He had apartment buildings in several cities within a 100-mile radius of his home. A property manager maintained and took care of the properties. He had a $5,000,000 umbrella liability policy which he and his CPA felt was more than enough. Every year for four years his attorney advised him to do advanced asset protection planning and every year he said, "sounds like a good idea, let me check with my CPA." His attorney would always respond, "I don't mean any disrespect, but what does your CPA know about asset protection?" The investor explained, "He has to file the taxes and fill out the forms, and he probably has some experience in this area. I just want to get his opinion." His CPA told him that asset protection planning beyond umbrella insurance wasn't necessary, and it would make his taxes more complex (he'd have two additional tax returns per year).

What happens to that real estate investor in the following scenario? This is a reprint from a 2015 article in the Los Angeles Times:

LOS ANGELES, CA --

A 13-year-old teenager may have been killed by carbon monoxide poisoning two days after Christmas. Kim Holt, who lost her daughter, now wants to make sure no one else loses a loved one. "Yesterday evening I got a call from the coroner saying that they hadn't done the autopsy yet, but there were high levels of carbon monoxide poisoning in her bloodstream," she said.

She said that her daughter, Zoey Hernandez, had been staying with a family friend for the last couple of months. They had just moved to a different home on the night that Zoey died.

"If there were the proper monitors up in each room like they're supposed to be then this just wouldn't have happened," Holt said.

Carbon monoxide detectors and alarms can play a vital role in preventing poisoning. In California, all single-family homes with an attached garage or a fossil fuel source are legally required to have a detector.

Los Angeles Fire Department spokesperson Margaret Stewart said carbon monoxide is a danger to millions of people, and it's the leading cause of unintentional poisoning across the U.S. "It's called the silent killer because it's odorless, colorless, tasteless. So it's invisible to us, so people don't know when they have an issue until they're already feeling symptoms," she said.

She added that there's an increase in cases during the winter months, especially when people without adequate heat start using whatever they can to stay warm. She warned that people should never try to heat their homes with an appliance, such as an oven or barbecue.

Holt said she is in unimaginable pain, but she wants to prevent others from having to experience it. "Three days ago, I had a little girl that was the world to me, and now she's gone because of this," she said.

What do you think the real estate investor's insurance company would say when the real estate owner files a claim regarding the above scenario? That's right, "Sorry, your policy has an exclusion for gross negligence and we believe you were grossly negligent. If you disagree, feel free to sue us." Of course, the insurance company would tie him up in court for years with their legal team, while his assets are taken by the child's family.

Or, how about my own experience relying on an insurance company? I used to be president of a technology company in San Francisco. We had to let one of our executives go and he sued us for wrongful termination. In my opinion, he had no case, but nevertheless we had to defend it. We turned the matter over to our liability insurance company. We weren't worried, we specifically had coverage for wrongful termination claims.

I will never forget the night before the trial. I was sitting in my office when an adjuster from the insurance company called me. They had been managing the litigation up to this point. The adjuster told me they were no longer going to pay for our defense and whatever the judgement was we were on our own. I read him the section of the policy where we were clearly covered. He was silent for a moment, then said, "Well, that is our opinion, if you believe we are wrong you are welcome to file a claim against us." I had the distinct impression he did this a lot.

So, there I was the night before trial, and I didn't have the time or money to sue a large insurance company with hundreds of lawyers. What did I do? I settled the next day before trial to minimize the company's risk. Even though our lawyers and I felt the ex-executive's case was a 100% loser, I couldn't take that risk. I had employees depending on me and a company to run.

In this instance, I was lucky. The claim wasn't so much that I couldn't settle for a reasonable amount, but I know of more than one example where this hasn't been the case, and the insurance company has found an exclusion (or at least said they have), leaving the business owner completely exposed.

If you are depending solely on umbrella liability insurance to protect you from lawsuits and creditors' claims, you are being foolish.

If your CPA or other advisors are saying you don't need asset protection beyond umbrella insurance, in my opinion, you should fire them immediately. It's that simple. They are being casual with your money and your family, and don't deserve your business. I work with some excellent CPAs and financial advisors, and I can tell you the good ones never counsel against protecting your assets. If a few more tax forms are overwhelming them, I know plenty of CPAs that can handle it and understand it's part of their job. They work alongside attorneys and are happy to help protect your assets - not expose them.

I never cease to be amazed when a successful business owner or real estate investor with a ten, twenty, thirty million dollars or more net worth comes to me asking me for asset protection advice, and they tell me they must "run it by their CPA". CPAs don't have any assets at risk. They don't have trucks, employees, customers that can get hurt or renters that can get injured on their property. So, you, the person who has built this empire, is going to a bookkeeper who has probably taken very little risk his or her entire life, for advice on how to protect your business? Does that make logical sense to you? Me neither, but it's why I now charge a lot of money to give asset protection advice. You can get bad advice for free, but remember, your CPA isn't going to lose anything when you get sued - you are!

Now, am I suggesting you shouldn't have umbrella insurance coverage? Of course not! It is often the first line of defense and can help pay legal fees in a lawsuit. However, when they call up the night before trial, as they did in my case, you better have a backup plan. Or, if the judgment exceeds the policy limits, you could lose everything and have your income garnished for the rest of your life. Do you really want to take that chance?

Business owners and professionals often tell me a few thousand dollars is too much too pay for asset protection. However, when they get sued and it is too late for me to help them, they are willing to pay almost any price. Don't be pennywise and pound foolish.

"It does not do to leave a live dragon out of your calculations, if you live near him."
~ J.R.R. Tolkien, The Hobbit

Chapter 4

Why LLCs, Corporations and Partnerships can be a Dangerous Trap in California

In the previous chapter hopefully you learned that relying on umbrella insurance by itself is not a wise choice. So, what should you have in addition to liability insurance then that will let you sleep soundly at night?

One thing you should consider is having an asset protection entity or two outside your business to protect your non-business assets and to protect your investment assets, like real estate, from causing you to lose personal assets, like your house or investment accounts.

As I mentioned earlier, entities like LLCs, corporations, and limited partnerships, have inside and outside liability. If you have an apartment building held by your LLC or LP, then it isolates that asset from your other assets. If something happens inside the LLC (like an apartment fire that harms someone) and your insurance doesn't come through, then only the apartment building inside the LLC is at risk (theoretically). Your assets outside the LLC are protected from what happened in that apartment building.

The reverse is also true. If something happens outside the LLC, in your business, for example, a creditor should not be able to take your apartment building, because it was owned by the separate LLC. (There are a variety of exceptions that can cause a court to unwind your planning, but those exceptions are beyond the scope of this book. We are going to assume you have planned properly, have the right language in your LLC operating agreement, and have followed the necessary formalities and laws for it to work well).

The LLC then, if formed and maintained correctly, isolates your assets from each other and essentially acts like a "moat" around each asset to prevent the "domino effect". The domino effect is when one asset causes a liability and that liability is big enough to put everything you own at risk. By segregating your assets properly, you are essentially putting enough space between your dominos so that they won't topple each other.

Now let's take the case of the investor with $15 million in real estate, liability insurance and three LLCs holding his rental properties. Assume he has three LLCs, each one holding six single family homes of roughly equivalent value ($5 million of real estate in each LLC, or roughly six properties worth approximately $833,000 each). Why does he have so many properties (six per LLC) exposed to each other in one LLC you might ask? Because he's too cheap to form more LLCs (it costs $800 a year in California to have an LLC and his CPA told him that was too much money - yes believe it or not I see this constantly in my practice).

So, in the scenario I gave you in the previous chapter, if one of the landlord's single-family residences was the scene of that young girl's death, what could happen? Let's assume the girl's family wins a ten million judgment due to projected loss of future earnings and other damages. The insurance company doesn't pay since they say you are grossly negligent. (Good luck suing them, but in the meantime the girl's family proceeds to collect their judgement).

Therefore, the girl's family is takes the six single family rental properties worth a total of five million ($5,000,000) that were all in the same LLC as the home the child died in (inside liability). That leaves you owing them $5,000,000 on the judgement. So where do they go to collect the additional $5 million?

Well, they could take your personal residence but for the sake of this example we're going to say you already live in Texas, so you have the full homestead exemption. The only assets you have left are the $10 million dollars of rental properties inside the two LLCs. Whew, you're safe, right? They can't take your other rental properties because the incident happened outside those two LLCs, right?

You are half right. We are assuming that they can't take the other single-family rental homes because the court won't let them. What remedy *can* they get? They can get what is called a "charging order." A charging order is an order by the court that says they are entitled to distributions (or in this case income) from the LLCs in satisfaction of the judgement. In other words, if the LLCs make money (which they probably do) the girl's family will be able to take the income from the LLCs until they have satisfaction of the claim.

Now there are a variety of things you can do to make it difficult on a creditor. You might decide to not distribute much cash this year and spend all the cash on property improvements. You can choose not to distribute anything and just hold on to it, but if you do that you still have to pay the taxes on the income earned and you won't have the cash distributed to do that. Of course, neither will the creditor, and perhaps that would make them want to settle if you have other resources to pay your taxes and they don't. However, all these games don't change the fact that a creditor can sit there and make your life miserable for as long as they have the patience to do so or until they get their money.

As you can see, an entity, like an LLC or a LP, doesn't give you total protection - only partial protection. You are basically hoping to use the entity as a negotiating ploy to persuade the creditor to settle for an amount less than the full claim. This is why relying upon entities alone for asset can be a trap for the unwary. It isn't a solution, only a negotiating tactic.

What about a corporation? Is that better? Unfortunately, no. A corporation in California can be dissolved and all assets given to a creditor. Hence, it is not a good idea to hold too many assets inside a corporation. You should hold real estate and equipment in an LLC or LP, and lease the real estate or equipment back to the corporation so that your assets are not exposed inside the corporation. The corporation is strictly to isolate your business liability from your personal liability.

Additionally, many litigators are experts at "piercing the corporate veil" and exposing your personal assets to liability, as well as your business assets. Piercing the corporate veil means you didn't follow all the formalities of a corporation (minutes, board meetings, resolutions for compensation and purchases, etc.), and therefore the court says the corporation was a sham and treats all your assets as one big pot available to creditors. One litigator I know says he estimates a minimum of 60% of private business owners do not follow the formalities necessary to maintain asset protection. Welcome to California!

You're saying, "But what about a Nevada LLC? I've heard those are better." Actually, in the above example I've presumed you used a Nevada LLC... and I've made an even bigger assumption. I've assumed that even though you don't have any relationship with Nevada other than this LLC (it's called nexus), and all the real estate is in California, for some reason a California court is going to let you control California property with an LLC in Nevada. Does that even start to make sense? No matter, I'm not even going to argue that here. I'm saving that for Chapter Nine of this book.

For the sake of argument, and to give the benefit of the doubt to Nevada attorneys, I am assuming a California court respects the Nevada LLC in this example. The Nevada LLC's sole remedy is a charging order, as I've described in the above case. Attorneys sell Nevada LLCs on the internet as if they have some magical power, but the reality is they are the same trap as any LLC. While it is true that the Nevada statutes say the courts can't dissolve an LLC and they can only issue a charging order, you can see a charging order is essentially a way to lock your property up for potentially years. Is that the kind of asset protection you're looking for? Can you do better? Yes, you can, if you have a business in California. A California business can do better than a charging order to protect your assets. You can use an exemption, and remember what I said about exemptions? Exemptions are *rights* and asset protections entities like LLCs, LPs, and domestic and offshore asset protection trusts, are *maybes*.

Section III
The Good News!

"Wise choices will watch over you."
~ Proverbs 2:11

Chapter 5
The California Advantage

W e've talked about the limitations of asset protection in California, and you've seen a comparison of California exemptions to other states. Are you ready to move?

Don't get the suitcases out of the closet just yet, because this chapter will let you sleep at night right where you're at. In the exemption chart from Chapter Two it was evident that Texas and Florida have a lot more asset exemptions than California. Yet, there was one thing that California has in that chart that those states don't: the private retirement plan.

What is the private retirement plan? It is an exemption created by the California Legislature in 1970. It is codified in the law under California Code of Civil Procedure § 704.115 as follows:

704.115. (a) As used in this section, private retirement plan means:

(1) Private retirement plans, including, but not limited to, union retirement plans.

(2) Profit-sharing plans designed and used for retirement purposes.

(3) Self-employed retirement plans and individual retirement annuities or accounts provided for in the Internal Revenue Code of 1986, as amended, including individual retirement accounts qualified under Section 408 or 408A of that code, to the extent

the amounts held in the plans, annuities, or accounts do not exceed the maximum amounts exempt from federal income taxation under that code.

(b) All amounts held, controlled, or in process of distribution by a private retirement plan, for the payment of benefits as an annuity, pension, retirement allowance, disability payment, or death benefit from a private retirement plan are exempt.

(c) Notwithstanding subdivision (b), where an amount described in subdivision (b) becomes payable to a person and is sought to be applied to the satisfaction of a judgment for child, family, or spousal support against that person:

(1) Except as provided in paragraph (2), the amount is exempt only to the extent that the court determines under subdivision (c) of Section 703.070.

As you can see from paragraph (c), there are some things a California private retirement plan does not protect you from, namely child and spousal support. What will it protect you from? Frivolous lawsuits from abusive customers, employees, and other undeserving creditors (except the IRS and Franchise Tax Board - sorry, it won't protect you from not paying your taxes). Finally, California has given us something that other states don't have! This is the reason for business owners to stay in California - so they can have this level of protection.

In plain English what is this code section saying? Simply stated it is saying that a California private retirement plan is exempt from creditors, and furthermore, a California private retirement plan is any private retirement plant that meets the following definition:

"All amounts held, controlled, or in process of distribution by a private retirement plan, for the payment of benefits as an annuity, pension, retirement allowance, disability payment, or death benefit from a **private retirement plan are exempt**."

Please note, this description does not mean it has to be an annuity, pension or disability payment, those are simply three of five options. The other two are: retirement allowance and death benefit.

It does *not* say in paragraph 3 that the plan must be an Individual Retirement Account as defined under 408 or 408A of the Internal Revenue Code. It simply says those can be included. In goes on in subsection b of paragraph 3 to specifically state what can qualify as a California private retirement plan in order to gain exempt status. As you can see, it expressly does not rely on ERISA for exempt status, and the fact that it states an ERISA plan can be (but does not have to be) included as a subset should clarify the legislative intent that the California private retirement plan has nothing to do with ERISA.

The California private retirement plan is a state right, not a federal right, and does not depend on federal law for its asset protection status. Federal law trumps state law except when it comes to property rights, where the Federal government accepts state law in most cases. For example, if you live in a community property state, the surviving spouse can save thousands of dollars on taxes over a surviving spouse in a separate property state, even though it is federal taxes.

To say that a California private retirement plan is not an ERISA plan is correct. To say that a California private retirement plan does not provide an exemption under state law to protect you from creditors and lawsuits is incorrect. The two are not related. It would be analogous to saying that the Texas or Florida or even California's homestead exemptions did not protect the equity in your home because they are not ERISA plans. What has ERISA got to do with a state mandated exemption right? Nothing. I suppose the fact that the word "retirement" is used is confusing to some people, but make no mistake, the California private retirement plan exemption is in addition to your Federal exemptions under ERISA. If you are not taking advantage of both your federal and California exemptions, you could be leaving a great part of your assets at risk to lawsuits and creditors. The following chapters will go into detail on how to maximize all your exemptions under federal and state law.

Is it that simple? Do you just have to say everything I own is now part of my California private retirement plan, and all your assets are protected? Of course not, although some people have tried that (to their misfortune).

Like many exemptions, which are rights under federal or state law, there are some things you must do to "claim" the exemption. In the case of a California private retirement plan you must do the following:

1. Qualify
2. Have a formal written and adopted private retirement plan
3. Not overfund the plan according to your current and future projected earnings
4. Properly maintain and administer the plan

I am going to get into the details of each of the above in Chapters Eight & Nine, and give some specific examples of properly structured California private retirement plans. The steps above are to illustrate that, like any good plan for the future, some effort is required. You can't just wish it into existence. If you do try and wish it so, and you get sued, you're going to be wishing you actually put some work in to set it up and maintain it properly. The good news is that, in my opinion, if you qualify, and you follow the rules I lay out in Chapter Nine, you are going to have the best asset protection you can get in California. The better news is you don't need tons of complicated entities to get it!

Now remember, the California retirement plan isn't new. This isn't some pie in the sky experiment I invented that I am just trying out. The California Legislature enacted the above statute in 1970, and as illustrated in the appendix, there is plenty of case law to show California courts respect this right. If you read the cases you will see the only times the California retirement plan was not respected by the courts is when it didn't follow the four principles I laid out above.

There is some confusion among lawyers and CPAs who refer to California retirement plans, and I think it is important to take a moment and clarify. When the California Legislature enacted this law, they had no intention to make this a tax deferred retirement plan like a 401(k) or IRA. In fact, this law was created *before* the federal retirement law (ERISA). When looking at the legislative history of ERISA, it is interesting to note the federal government studied California's private retirement plan legislation as a model for ERISA law.

The California private retirement plan has nothing to do with taxes (which I'll talk about more in the next chapter). It is tax neutral and it works like a pass-through entity. It was designed strictly to protect the retirement savings of qualified Californians who followed the law in setting up, funding, and properly maintaining a private retirement plan.

As mentioned earlier, the legislature never intended it to be an ERISA plan (how could they, since it was adopted four years prior to ERISA). It was meant to be as a legal exemption under California law for protecting your retirement assets. However, even though it is not an ERISA plan, it can be used in conjunction with ERISA plans to protect your assets. The fact that it is not an ERISA plan does not mean it is not protected like one, it simply means it offers none of the tax deferral of ERISA plans, which is actually a good thing. If I'm not asking the government to give me a tax break, that means I have a lot more flexibility as to what type of assets I can have in my California private retirement plan.

So, the fact that the California private retirement plan is tax neutral is a positive, because it allows you to combine your federal and state exemption rights for greater asset protection. It allows you more flexibility in your company as to who is eligible for the plan (could be just the owner), and it allows more investment options inside the plan (including letting you continue to fund your business growth with plan assets or investing in real estate).

Please see the appendix for a special FAQ section, prepared courtesy of Trust-CFO^{TM}, the third-party administrator I use for my clients when setting up and administrating a California private retirement plan.

"No enemy is worse than bad advice."
~ Sophocles

Chapter 6
Why Your Advisors Didn't Tell You

By now, you must be asking, "If the California private retirement plan is such a great deal then why haven't my CPA, financial advisor, or lawyer told me about it?" Before I show you how to structure an extremely effective and simple California private retirement and overall asset protection plan, it is probably worth explaining why you've never heard of this before. Unfortunately, these same people who are not telling you now are the same ones that will try and prevent you from implementing it in the future. You deserve to know better.

The fact that the California retirement plan is tax neutral is great for many reasons. It allows for more flexibility in who you include in the plan. It could be just you, you and your partners, or you and key executives. Not everyone is required to participate to have a plan. For example, I have a business client with three successful owners, where two owners have a California private plan and the other owner does not. This allows for greater flexibility than an ERISA plan, where you must include all your employees. Also, because you aren't asking for a tax break, you have more flexibility on what you can invest within the plan. You can invest the money back in the business, you can buy real estate, or almost anything that makes financial sense can be utilized. So, the tax neutrality of the private retirement plan is a great thing, right? Except it's also probably the number one reason you haven't about it!

There is nothing in the California private retirement plan that a financial advisor, insurance agent, or other investment professional can make money on. Since it is tax neutral, your CPA probably hasn't even heard about it. It's not on the CPA exam, and there is no tax planning involved.

Unlike your 401(k) plan where your financial advisor can charge a fee for managing assets, you're not required to have a financial advisor for your California private retirement plan. You can fund your California private retirement plan with your company stock or with your personal real estate investments to protect from lawsuits either in or outside your business. Can you have a financial advisor? Can you have stocks and mutual funds? Sure, but you aren't *required* to, and since this plan is limited to California the big national mutual fund companies that are inside 401(k) plans (such as Fidelity, Schwab, Merrill Lynch, Vanguard, etc.) do not bother marketing a specific California private retirement plan. They don't know how, and they aren't lawyers, so they aren't selling legal solutions - just mutual funds.

If it's a legal solution, and not a tax or financial solution, why hasn't your lawyer told you about it? I don't know the definitive answer but there are many theories.

Remember, it's a state exemption and state exemptions are unique to each state, so it is not something they teach in law school. I never had a class in "asset protection." Most law schools do teach entity formation, but few, if any, teach asset protection by itself. I'm sure you've heard the expression "if all you have is a hammer, everything looks like a nail."

Many "asset protection" attorneys are what I call "national experts." They practice in multiple states, or as is often the case, they are promoting the asset protection features of their state to multiple jurisdictions (for example, the Nevada LLC). Again, this is more of the "if you only have a hammer" mentality. Since they don't practice in California and are trying to sell more of what they do offer, why in the world would they want you to have a California private retirement plan (assuming they even knew about it)? Even if the "national experts" who write books are licensed and practice in California, why would they want to promote a California private retirement plan? There just isn't that much money in it for the attorney.

The California private retirement plan is not the solution I make the most money on. Most of the work to set up and maintain a California private retirement plan is performed by a third-party administrator (TPA). I can make much more money setting up multiple and layered entities, as well as drafting complex operating agreements and multiple irrevocable trusts. Believe it or not some attorneys want to make money (hard to believe, I know).

I recently set up an elaborate asset protection plan for a wealthy client, to protect his real estate investments and personal assets. I drafted and implemented multiple entities and layered them to provide levels of protection. I recommended a more effective plan that was less complex and less expensive, but his financial advisor and CPA were not familiar with the California private retirement plan. I try and educate my clients and give them options, but if they want to listen to the advice of out-of-date advisors there is only so much I can do. If I hadn't developed the plan recommended by the advisors they would have sent him to another attorney, and I would have lost a client.

As an attorney, I can make thousands more in fees selling off shore trusts, multiple entity planning, and any number of other more complicated solutions than the California private retirement plan. So why am I telling you about it, you might ask? I've been doing this long enough to know that 90% of the business owners and professionals who read this still won't have the confidence to overrule their CPA and financial advisor, even when an experienced attorney is telling them the opposite. I feel an obligation to give you good information, and this book is my way of doing that. I have done what I believe is my ethical and moral duty, but I have no duty to make decisions for you. I will say this, however, the 10% of business owners that make their own decisions and know when to overrule bad advice, are the ones who most often accelerate to the next level.

Section IV
Best Practices in California

"Surely there comes a time when counting the cost and paying the price aren't things to think about any more. All that matters is value."
~ James Hilton

Chapter 7

How to Set Up a California Private Retirement Plan That Works

In my opinion, if there is one problem with the California private retirement plan, it is that the code section 704.115 does not go into enough detail. Therefore, over the years we have had various cowboys try and abuse it.

The code is clear on stating categorically that assets in a California private retirement plan are exempt when one has a legitimate plan and properly recharacterizes funded assets, but the code does not specify how much or what types of assets may be funded, as long as they are legitimate for retirement. However, as I said earlier, this is not cutting-edge law. It has been around for over 45 years and only updated by the legislature in 1991. Hence, there has been plenty of case law developed around California private retirement plans to tell us what works and what doesn't. Based on the statute, the legislative history, and the case law, the following elements are what I believe to be essential to ensure your plan will exempt your assets from creditors. I will list them and then discuss each one:

1. Third-party administrator (TPA)
2. Qualification diagnosis by the TPA (do you qualify?)
3. Asset exemption analysis by the TPA (which of your assets are eligible for exemption)
4. Funding analysis based on income, age, and retirement needs
5. Plan documentation and funding of plan

6. Annual administration and review
7. Independent trustee

These are all critical steps, because if you are ever sued, opposing counsel is going to argue that your plan did not meet one or more or even all of these requirements. In the appendix you will find a few cases where a court allowed a creditor access to assets in a "so-called" California private retirement plan, due to not following requirements. Often there was no third-party administrator, no diagnostic, no funding analysis, no annual administration, inadequate plan documentation, and very little effort to maintain the plan requirements. It really isn't that difficult to make the plan work, but like anything else, if you try and cut corners you put everything at risk.

1. **Third-Party Administrator**: The good news is that all the requirements I am giving, all the details and all the worry, are not done by you! You outsource to an expert that knows what to do and when and how to do it. They take care of the following steps. The bad news is, when you try to do this by yourself, as some losing cases in the appendix will demonstrate, you are probably not going to like the outcome. It amazes me that business owners and professionals with millions of dollars of assets at risk will attempt to do things on their own to save money, and in the process put everything at risk. Don't make that mistake. Don't assume your current 401(k) administrator is going to know what you're talking about. I will give more information on how to choose a good TPA in the next few pages, but whoever you choose, make sure they are experienced with the California retirement plan.

2. **Qualification Diagnostics**: Not everyone is going to qualify for a California private retirement plan, so it is important you have the third-party administrator (TPA) complete a diagnostic of your situation. Here are the factors they look at:

   a. Current age
   b. Income
   c. If you have a business
   d. Projected retirement age

     e. Projected retirement income needs

     f. Balance sheet both business and personal

     g. Current retirement assets

Don't jump to conclusions about whether you qualify or not based on assumptions. For example, if you are 62 and want to retire in 3 years, you still might qualify due to a variety of other factors. The diagnostic only takes a few minutes and I will tell you how to do one privately on your own at the end of this chapter.

It's often easier to determine who *isn't* a candidate. For example, if you are an executive working for a corporation and your only source of income is on a W-2 and a large 401(k), you probably won't qualify because your retirement needs are taken care of by the 401(k). You also don't have a lot of exposure on your assets because your company is at risk, not you. However, if you are an executive with a W-2 and personal real estate investment holdings generating significant income, you may qualify, as your retirement income needs are based on more than your salary, and you have significant assets at risk.

The ideal candidate for a California private retirement plan is a business owner, or professional (doctor, lawyer, engineer, farmer, rancher, financial advisor, etc.), making a minimum of $300,000 a year from their business or practice. He or she would have personal or business assets at risk, which if lost to a creditor would interfere with their ability to retire.

Even if you do not have a business or professional practice, you may qualify if you are an investor with significant assets at risk, such as investment real estate or a stock portfolio. For example, I have one client that qualified even though his only business was real estate investing. He owned $10,000,000 worth of rental property, which if he lost would mean he could never retire and would have to start over in life. He was a perfect candidate, even though he was close to retirement age and did not own a "business" employing other people. In fact, one of the many good things about the California private retirement plan is there is no requirement to have employees, and should you have employees, there is no requirement to include them in the plan.

3. **Asset Exemption Analysis:** Also done by a TPA, this analysis shows which of your assets, if any, can be used to fund the California private retirement plan, and can therefore be protected from lawsuits. This is a critical step, because as explained earlier, exemption is better than asset transfers for protecting you from lawsuits and creditors.

    Remember, the California private retirement plan can exempt more than just your business assets - it can also exempt your non-business investment or personal assets, if it is determined those assets are necessary to fund your retirement. If you own a business and you have an apartment building or single-family home that you rent out as an investment, and the equity in that real estate is needed to fund your retirement, those non-business assets can also be incorporated into the plan and exempted. Even if you have no assets outside the business other than your home, the equity in your home could be incorporated into the plan if the analysis indicates you will need that equity in retirement.

4. **Funding Analysis:** This is a part of the asset exemption analysis, but goes further to project the annual funding requirement needed for your retirement plan. For example, if you make $300,000 annually from your business, and you want to retire in 10 years, it will determine how much you need to put into the plan each year to meet your required retirement income. The nice thing about the California retirement plan, as opposed to a plan like ERISA (a defined benefit plan), is if you can't fund it in a particular year due to a business downturn the plan is not terminated. This is why you have funded the plan with other assets, as a funding guarantee. California recognized that business is not always a straight line, and that some years are better than others.

    Another great thing about the California private retirement plan is the flexibility. The money you put into your California retirement plan can continue to be used to capitalize and grow the business. It is not locked up in low return mutual funds where you can't access the money (remember, this is one of the reasons no one has told you about it - they can't make any money off you). You can borrow money from your own private bank that protects your savings for retirement from creditors and lawsuits. It is the best of all possible worlds; you protect your money *and* maintain flexibility regarding investments. You can invest into your business, real estate, or stocks and bonds if you want to. While you are not the trustee of the plan, you can still direct investments as long as they further your goals towards retirement.

5. **Plan Documentation and Funding:** This is a critical step that is often overlooked or done incorrectly. Not only should your company have an overall plan document that clearly lays out the plan parameters and guidelines, but each plan participant needs their own trust to hold and protect plan assets. Without proper documentation, it is hard to make an argument you meant to have a plan. Your plan administrator can help you with this. They have certain guidelines that must be in the documents and work with attorneys that know the requirements. It is important to understand that not all third-party administrators are qualified to be TPAs for a California private retirement plan, and very few lawyers are familiar with the drafting requirements. Also, third-party administrators for the California private retirement plan are few and far between because they tend to like plans where they can manage money in mutual funds. There is very little effort on their part with traditional ERISA plans, as the actual money management is done by a large company that manages the mutual funds (i.e. Fidelity or Vanguard).

I work with TRUST-CFO™ as my third-party administrator. They were the first to focus on the California private retirement plan, which they have trademarked as the California Private Retirement Trust™, and they have developed a suite of unique proprietary tools from initial diagnostics to annual review and maintenance. Together we make sure that every item on the list of requirements for a valid plan are designed and implemented. In fact, you can even use their diagnostic tool at www.trust-cfo.com to quickly see if you are qualified to set up a California Private Retirement Trust™. Feel free to type in my name, Reed Scott, as the referral source when filling out the page to see if you qualify. Make sure to scroll to the bottom of the page and hit the submit button, then wait to make sure it has taken your submission before leaving the page. You will get an email back with the summary results. If you qualify, you can contact TRUST-CFO™ directly or you can email me at reed@yesllp.com for more information.

Whomever you work with, make sure they have experience with the California private retirement plan under CCP § 704.115. This is not a commodity, you won't find it at LegalZoom, and unless your attorney has experience with asset protection planning they will probably not be familiar with the requirements of the plan.

6. **Annual Administration and Review:** Another reason to use a third-party administrator is the need for your plan to have annual reviews and modifications, and stay consistent with changes in your life, your retirement goals, and in the environment. For example, the present rate of inflation is low and therefore a lower rate of return on assets is used to calculate your retirement needs. As inflation starts to creep back into our economy, however, your plan will need to be recalculated to stay compliant. This is just one example of many, but again these requirements are things you don't need to worry about. Your TPA will work on this crucial element of protection behind the scenes.

    Additionally, your TPA makes sure your plan is always in compliance with the plan requirements. They document all transactions and compile that information for annual reporting and review.

7. **Independent Trustee:** The trust for your California private retirement plan must have an independent trustee who is not related to you or under your control. This is part of what enables the asset protection of the plan. I have seen people use a sibling as trustee, but it's hard to make the case your brother or sister is an independent trustee. Again, this is not something you need to worry about. When you use a qualified TPA like TRUST-CFO™, they have licensed, insured professional attorney trustees that can be the trustee of your plan. There are many safeguards in place to make sure the trustee does their job, including insurance and trust protectors who can fire the trustee and replace them if they are not following plan guidelines.

"Simple can be harder than complex: You have to work hard to make it simple. But it's worth it in the end because once you get there you can move mountains."
~ Steve Jobs

Chapter 8
Complexity and Limited Protection vs. Simplicity and Effectiveness

Attorneys like to sound intelligent. We like the sound of our own voice, especially if we can talk about stuff most people aren't familiar with. The more complexity we can throw in the mix the bigger the bill. Now I'm not saying attorneys do that on purpose, but it sure seems that way sometimes, even to another attorney!

Realistically, most attorneys are highly ethical and moral people who just happen to like complexity. Most of my clients on the other hand, are successful business people who must make quick decisions on limited information, and they like it simple. This is a dilemma because some of the asset protection techniques that are currently in use by attorneys are incredibly complex, and in my opinion, of limited effectiveness.

In this chapter I'm going to give you two visual examples. The first example is the traditional asset protection plan used today by most asset protection attorneys to protect business owners and professionals. Remember, this book is for those who have had the talent and good fortune to accumulate significant assets in California, not Texas, not Florida, and not Nevada. You would have different options if you lived there, but you don't, so we're not discussing them.

In Chapter One I talked about the unreliable protection offered by asset protection entities such as limited partnerships and limited liability companies, but it bears repeating. In the following examples you will see that not only are traditional planning vehicles like corporations, limited partnerships and limited liability companies extremely complex, but they are also of limited effectiveness.

Let's take the following situation and see how it would be handled with traditional asset transfers and entity protection, rather than simpler and more streamlined exemption planning.

Bob Smith, a 55-year-old construction company owner, approaches his business or estate planning attorney and says: "I've got a successful company with 100 employees. I've been in business 20 years and I personally make $600,000 a year from the business. I have also invested in real estate and I have acquired 12 single family homes that I rent out as investment property. I max out my contribution to my 401(k) profit sharing plan, but other than that I don't have any retirement savings. I'm counting on the real estate to provide for my retirement once all the mortgages are paid off."

Bob is concerned because his friend, who also owns a construction business, just got hit with a $2,000,000 personal judgement for violation of the California wage and labor regulations (for not giving his employees adequate overtime). Bob worries, "If that happens to me and they come after my personal assets, I'll be in bad shape. I won't have time to rebuild my assets. My friend was innocent, and his employees didn't take breaks when they were told. They violated his rules and policies and he didn't even know it. He couldn't be on every jobsite at every minute."

On the next page, see what Bob's attorney comes up with as his "asset protection" plan:

TYPICAL ASSET PROTECTION DIAGRAM

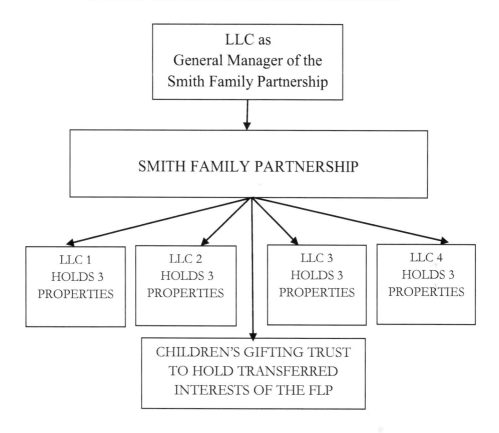

Here we have 7 separate entities set up by the attorney. To start, there is a family limited partnership (FLP) so Bob can transfer interests in his assets to his kids, because his attorney recommended bringing in other partners (besides himself and his wife) for the best asset protection. His attorney explained the more partners he had, the better the protection because it would appear more "legitimate" to the courts. They would also be less likely to take Bob's assets, because the courts don't want to penalize other partners for the bad behavior of just one partner. That made sense to Bob.

He didn't want to transfer the interest in the family limited partnership outright into each kid's name, because his sons were married, and he didn't want his daughters-in-law having a say in his business. So, he transferred the interests in the FLP to an irrevocable gifting trust. This trust held the FLP interests in the name of the trust, for the benefit of the kids. This way, the kids owned the FLP interests, but Bob was still in charge because of his "trustee" status, and he decided how the interests would vote or receive assets.

So now we have two entities, the FLP and the irrevocable gifting trust, but there's more. Bob has 12 single family homes, and if you remember from Chapter One, if all the homes are in one partnership or LLC they are all exposed to something that happens to one. The LLC or limited partnership (LP) isolates the rental property from your personal assets, like your home, but it doesn't keep someone from taking an investment property, if an incident leading to a claim happened on that property. Additionally, unless the property where the incident happened is isolated from your other investment properties, the claimant can go after those as well. This means that for the best and highest level of protection Bob should put each single-family home in a separate LLC. This will isolate each property from every other property, and at most a claimant inside one LLC can only take one property.

Even though that sounds like good advice, Bob's CPA suggests it would be too expensive and he should just get more insurance instead of creating multiple LLCs. Bob is dubious, because his friend who had the $2,000,000 judgement had insurance and it didn't cover him. Even though he wanted the best protection, he didn't like the idea that he had to pay the state of California $800 a year for each LLC because that would be $9,600 ($800 x 12=$9,600) so he thought he would half-listen to his CPA and only get 4 LLCs instead. He would put 3 properties in each LLC; this way if something happened on one property he would only lose three properties (the one where the incident occurred and the other two that were exposed because they were inside the same LLC).

If we assume that each single-family home is worth $350,000, then each LLC would have approximately $1.050 million worth of assets inside it. As there are 3 properties inside each LLC, that means there is an extra $700,000 at risk and exposed to a claim on another property (2 x $350K = $700K). If we take $700K of extra exposure multiplied by 4 (the number of LLCs), that equals $2,800,000 of Bob's assets exposed to a claim on a different property. Bob saved $6,400 a year in LLC fees by setting up 4 instead 12, but he exposed $2.8 million of property as a result. So, by exposing $2.8 million of his assets to a lawsuit, Bob saved .002% a year ($6,400/$2,800,000=.002).

That doesn't sound like a great asset protection plan, does it? Just wait, it gets worse. Let's now assume Bob gets sued not for something that happens on his property, but instead with a claim similar to what happened with his friend. The California Department of Labor files a wage and hour claim against him. His insurance doesn't cover him, because he broke the law. So, he gets a $2,000,000 personal judgement against him. The state goes after his rental properties in the LLCs, and get a judgement against them as well. The court dissolves the LLCs and claims he didn't set them up and maintain them properly, and therefore they are a sham. Therefore, the court thinks a charging order is an insufficient remedy and they dissolve the LLCs, and lets the state take 6 of Bob's properties to cover the judgment.

"But," you say, "I thought the only remedy an outside creditor can get against an LLC is a charging order, and they would have to wait for Bob to make a profits distribution. Can't Bob decide not to make a profits distribution, and make the creditor negotiate?" Unfortunately, the state of California is creditor friendly and does not always respect a charging order as the only remedy. The court can dissolve LLCs if they "believe" it is an appropriate remedy.

"Aha!" you exclaim, "I don't have Bob's problem. *My* attorney is very smart. He used Nevada LLCs, and everyone knows in Nevada the charging order is the only remedy and the court doesn't have an option." Sounds good, except for the facts - if the property is situated in California, the courts apply California law. They don't care where the LLC is from. In *Butler v. Adoption Media*, 486 F. Supp. 2d 1022 (N.D. Cal. 2007), California law was applied to a non-California LLC concerning matters of limited liability between the LLC and an unrelated third party.

So, even if Bob went to the "asset protection" expert from Nevada who made their entities sound invincible, he could still get an order charged right up his assets. Still want a Nevada attorney giving you advice on how to protect your California assets?

Presumably, Bob probably paid his attorney between $20,000 to $40,000 to set up the FLP and LLCs in the first place. Then he paid $3,200 a year to the state for the LLC tax ($800 per year per LLC) and he had 5 additional tax returns.

So, were Bob's assets protected? It doesn't look like it. A better question might be, what value did Bob receive for all that money and complexity in his life? I also must mention there was actually even more complexity. The FLP needed a general partner, because a family limited partnership is required to have one, so the attorney made another of the LLCs the general partner of the FLP, to limit Bob's exposure. Additionally, with the above asset protection scheme, Bob couldn't put his home in an LLC to protect it, but he was anxious of losing his residence of 20 years. His attorney told him the only way to protect the home was a qualified personal residence trust (QPRT), essentially an irrevocable trust to protect Bob's home from creditors. Two more tax returns.

Let's review: initial set up cost, anywhere from $20,000 to $40,000, plus $7,000 in annual fees for state tax and tax reporting on each entity. For that all Bob got was ineffective complexity!

The California Private Retirement Plan

So, what *should* Bob do? Sell everything and move his cash to an offshore trust in the Cook Islands? He could do that for set up fees closer to $50,000, plus annual trust administration fees between 1 and 2.5 % every year, paid to an offshore bank as trustee. However, he can't move more than half his assets offshore, or that would be a voidable transfer. Since Bob is making a killing in real estate, he also doesn't like the limited investment options with the offshore bank. He still wants to be in control. Come on Bob, you can't have your cake and eat it too. Actually... he can.

Here's what Bob's asset protection looks like with a well designed and implemented California private retirement plan:

CALIFORNIA PRIVATE RETIREMENT PLAN

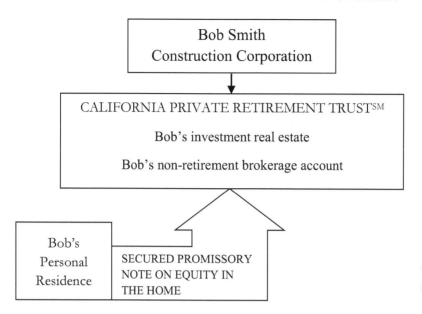

As you can see Bob's California private plan exempts his assets that aren't already exempt. In other words, Bob has $1,000,000 in a 401(k) that is already exempt under federal ERISA law, so we don't need to protect it. However, Bob's real estate investments worth $4,200,000 and his personal residence with equity of $1,000,000 is fully exposed to lawsuits and creditors. How can we protect these assets without a complex, hard to maintain, multi-entity asset protection plan like in the previous section, which did not really offer much protection anyway?

We protect Bob's assets by using his state exemption under CCP § 704.115, and set up his exempt California private retirement plan.

The first thing we must do, however, is determine which assets are eligible for protection for Bob's retirement. I am going to simplify this example for illustrative purposes, but if you want a detailed analysis of your own exemption rights I recommend you go to www.Trust-CFO.com and use their diagnostic tool. In Bob's case, his annual income from the business is $600,000 and Bob has only $1,000,000 in his 401(k). Assuming Bob would like to maintain close to his current standard of living when he retires in 10 years at 65, he would need to make at least 85% of $600,000 in annual income or $510,000 (for the purposes on this illustration I am ignoring inflation, but it is built into the diagnostic at www.Trust-CFO.com).

Assuming Bob can get a 4% return on his money (which is what most financial advisors would tell you is a reasonable number), Bob would get $40,000 a year in income from his present 401(k) amount of $1,000,000. Remember, Bob's 401(k) is his only protected retirement asset currently, so it is all he can really count on for his retirement. His other assets, his real estate investments and his home (except for his $100k California homestead exemption), can be taken from him at any time. Therefore, he can't count on those assets for retirement.

How much does Bob need to have in his California private retirement plan to ensure he can live at even 85% of his current standard of living? Assuming he needs $510,000 and assuming he can earn 4% annual return on his money, which is a reasonable assumption given today's rates, he will need to protect $12,750,000 for his retirement ($510,000/.04=$12,750,000)!

That's a lot of money, and it doesn't even put Bob at the same standard of living he has today. This means we can exempt up to $11,750,000 of Bob's current assets to make sure his retirement is protected as he is entitled under state law ($12,750,000 - $1,000,000 current exempt 401(k) = $11,750,000). Bob does not have $12,750,000 of assets currently, which means we can exempt almost all of his current assets and still have room for Bob to accumulate and protect more for his retirement. Again, note that I did not include an inflation adjustment. When your third-party administrator does the actual analysis, they will build in a reasonable inflation adjustment, which means the amount needed for retirement could be significantly higher.

Based on this analysis, you can see from the exemption diagnostic summary results report below that we can exempt all of Bob's $4,200,000 of investment real estate, his stock portfolio, and the cash value of his insurance, as well as secure the equity in his home of $1,000,000 against future funding, and still have $4,915,975 of assets that could be exempted for additional growth within Bob's exempt California retirement plan ($11,750,000 -$4,200,000-$1,000,000-500,000-50,000=$4,915,975 amount left that could be exempted).

The summary report below demonstrates that before utilizing the California private retirement plan, 86% of Bob's assets, both business and personal, were exposed to creditors. After creating and properly funding his California private retirement plan, only 16.3% of Bob's assets are available to creditors!

Bear in mind that the summary report below is only part of the analysis that must be completed to fully understand Bob's eligibility for the plan. Trying to do this on your own, without a third-party administrator who understands the process and ongoing annual adjustments required to keep the plan current, is why some plans have failed. If I have to defend your plan against creditor attacks, I want to show a judge that we followed proper procedures for funding and maintaining your plan.

EXEMPTION DIAGNOSTIC - SUMMARY RESULTS REPORT

Client	Bob Smith	
Age	55	
Retirement Age	65	
Taxable Income	$ 600,000.00	

	Current Exposed Plan	Proposed Exemption Plan
Net Worth	$ 8,165,000	$ 8,165,000
Homestead Exemption	$ 100,000	$ 100,000
Qualified ERISA Exemption	$ 1,000,000	$ 1,000,000
Life Insurance Net Cash Values	$ 25,600	$ 50,000
Real Estate	$ -	$ 4,200,000
Private Investments/Portfolios	$ -	$ 500,000
Business Equity	$ 15,675	$ 984,025
Exempt Asset Values:	$ 1,141,275	$ 6,834,025
Net Estate Exposure	$ 7,023,725	$ 1,330,975
Lifetime Creditor Exposure	86.0%	16.3%
Exempt Life Ins. Death Benefits	$ -	$ 2,000,000
TOTAL Creditor Exemption Benefits	$ 1,141,275	$ 8,834,025
Annual Tax Exemption Funding	$ -	$ 150,000
Tax Rate		53.0%
Annual Tax Exemption Savings	$ -	$ 79,500
TOTAL Tax Exemption Benefits	$ -	$ 795,000

So, how much did Bob have to pay for his California private retirement plan, which offers a state exemption from creditors as opposed to limited protection from an LLC?

I can't speak for other attorneys, but in the above scenario I would estimate that Bob's one time set up fees would be approximately $7,500, and his annual fees thereafter would be approximately $7,500. That's about $12,000 to $20,000 less than the complex and inefficient multiple entity scheme in the previous example! The annual fees are about the same, but the level of complexity has gone down exponentially. More importantly, we now have assets which are exempt and unavailable to creditors, as opposed to being held hostage by a creditor with a charging order. In Bob's California private retirement plan he now only has one additional tax return every year, instead of six. And instead of six separate bank accounts that he would need for each entity in the previous example, he has only one additional.

Perhaps the best news is that Bob can continue to use the money in his California private retirement plan the way he wants. He can invest in real estate, he can invest back in his business, he can buy stocks and bonds, insurance, annuities, or anything that can help him fund his retirement.

The big question is, though, does it work? Does the state exemption under CCP§ 704.115 really protect Bob's assets? How come you haven't heard about it? Well, in Chapter Six I already gave my opinion why you haven't heard about it, and why you probably will continue to not hear about it. Don't take my word for it though, read the cases in Appendix A. Those cases will demonstrate how the California retirement plan works if structured properly. It will also show how it will *not* work if you don't follow the rules. There are over 47 years of legislative and case law history on the California private retirement plan.

Make a decision to protect yourself, and make sure it is informed.

Chapter 9
Overall Reasonableness

If I could identify one thing that causes people to fail in creating a California private retirement plan, or any asset protection plan for that matter, it would have to be greed.

I think you too will realize this phenomenon when you examine the cases in the appendix where the courts did not respect the owner's plan. Usually, you can count on one of four things: 1. A qualified TPA and attorney were not hired to set up proper plan documentation and guidelines; 2. He/she had no analysis to determine what could be put in the plan based on their unique circumstances; 3. The owner blatantly tried to defraud creditors by setting up the plan at the last minute, with no forethought as to how much they actually needed in retirement; and, 4. There was no annual review, analysis, reporting, or formal administration of the plan.

Using the facts and evidence, the court will analyze whatever planning you have based upon a reasonableness test. Whether it is a California private retirement plan, a family limited partnership, a limited liability company or some other entity, most judges look for evidence of whether you used sound and reasonable judgement in your actions. If you qualify, and follow the steps laid out in Chapter Seven, I believe the California private retirement plan offers the highest level of protection with the least cost and complexity.

Now does this mean that I wouldn't also advise other types of asset protection and entity formation for my clients? Of course not! Each client is unique, and I base my recommendations on their specific goals and circumstances. There are still plenty of reasons to set up entities. For example, I often set up family limited partnerships because the operating agreement allows us to bring in other partners and family members. We can allocate taxes differently among the partners, we can allow for basis adjustment among partners or any variety of other planning considerations. The same holds true for limited liability companies, which can be taxed as a partnership, and S-corporation or a disregarded entity for a married couple or single person.

In addition, if you have more assets than can be protected in a California private retirement plan, how do you protect the excess? This is where I often recommend a charitable LLC in combination with a California private retirement plan. This level of asset protection goes above and beyond the traditional LLC, and if done properly, the tax benefits could pay for your planning fees and much more. The charitable LLC is one of my favorite tax and asset protection planning entities, and I have included a summary of how it works in Chapter Eleven of this book. For those investors or business owners who wish for more detail please feel free to email me at rscott@yesllp.com.

The purpose of this book is not to claim one size fits all and that there is only one type of planning for asset protection. On the contrary, it is to introduce the California business person and professional to a right and an exemption they have under California law that they are typically unaware of, in the hopes it can help them sleep soundly in this crazy, litigious world we live in called California.

Lastly, I want to talk about the one subject that seems to get everyone's attention - taxes! It is amazing how much time and effort people put into complaining about their taxes, and yet I can't get them to implement any of a number of simple solutions that can save them literally hundreds of thousands of dollars on their annual tax bill. It's like the weather, people talk about it, but no one does anything about it... except unlike the weather, I can actually do something about your tax bill!

Section V
Coordinated Tax and Asset Protection Planning

"Information is power, particularly when the competition ignores the opportunity to do the same."
~ Mark Cuban

Chapter 10
Tax Credits - What Are You Leaving on the Table?

I'm going to give you 5 simple tax savings tips in this chapter that I hope you've heard about, but if you haven't you may be leaving significant dollars on the table instead of your pocket. If you haven't heard of them and want to learn more feel free to email me at reed@yesllp.com.

Federal Work Opportunity Tax Credit "WOTC"

This wage based tax credit is available for all US taxpayers and the credit is for a business when it hires a "qualified" individual. The wage credit is based on 40% of the first $6,000 of wages for a qualified new hire which is capped at $2,400 in the year of hire.

Qualified employees are those collecting federal assistance such as SNAP (which benefits 70 million people in the US), recently separated Veterans from our armed forces, felons, and those that are long term unemployed (defined at 28 weeks prior to date of hire). The trick with this credit, is you must capture the new employee data within 30 days of date of hire. If you're thinking how in the world would you know this information when hiring, know that there are companies that can help you take advantage of the credit. Obviously, this credit isn't for everyone, but if you hire seasonally or have high turnover then this credit could be a real competitive advantage for your business and real money in your pocket.

Federal Empowerment Zone Tax Credit – "FEZ"

This federal tax credit is location based as the business and its employees must be located within the FEZ. A federal credit of up to $3,000 per qualified employee can be claimed for each tax year. The FEZ technically expired in 2016, however, there may be refund opportunities for you for the past 3 years. A recently implemented FEZ study for an apparel manufacturer with 120 employees created about $75,000 in refunds.

California New Employment Credit "NEC"

This credit replaced the former Enterprise Zone Tax Credit and is effective through December 31, 2021. The taxpayer's business must be located within the "Designated Geographic Area" (DGA) and is basically the same as the former Enterprise Zone Locations. DGA cities in Northern and Central California include:

Bakersfield
Delano
Eureka
Fresno
Kings County
Madera
Modesto
Merced
Oakland
Pittsburg
Pittsburg-Bay Point
Porterville
Richmond
Sacramento
San Francisco
San Jose
San Joaquin
Shafter
Siskiyou
Stanislaus

Taft
Watsonville
Yuba/Sutter

The wage credit is equal to the excess paid for hourly wages over $15 and under $35 per hour multiplied by 35% for 5 years. So, for an admin person making $50k per year, the business would get approximately $7,000 in a California tax credit in year one and potentially $35,000 over 5 years.

Employees must be qualified on the date of hire, based on the following criteria:

a) Long term unemployed (26 weeks)
b) Claimed the earned income credit on 1040
c) Collecting state assistance such as SNAP or AFDC (Aid to Families with Dependent Children)
d) Felon
e) Recently separated veteran

The program runs very similar to WOTC above and you must file applications with the FTB within 30 days of date of hire. And, yes, you can collect both federal and state hiring credits if you are in the right "zone."

These are often overlooked incentives for business owners in retail, restaurants, distribution, auto dealerships and generally any that pay minimum wage. These incentives can easily add up to six figures annually.

Research and Development Credits

This federal and California tax credit is available for business that conduct research, process improvement and product development activities. Qualified Research Activities "QRE" can include business from manufacturers to software developers and everything in between. Recent legislation has made qualifying for the R&D Credit more favorable for businesses and there may be refund opportunities for you. A $30M construction client with 200 employees recently had an R&D

study done and more than $400,000 in federal and state tax credits were found.

Cost Segregation

If a business owns real estate or if you have a rental property that you paid more than $1M for, you may qualify for a Cost Segregation Study. Cost Segregation is an engineered based study that looks at the components of your building, such as windows, flooring, lighting, HVAC and more. The study will support a one-time catch up tax deduction which is taken in the current tax year, and can substantially reduce or eliminate your federal and California current year tax liability. A $40M manufacturing company recently did a Cost Segregation Study on their headquarters building and found an additional $500,000 of deductible depreciation.

Again, if you're wondering how you actually do this, don't worry, there are engineering and accounting firms that know and will document everything for the IRS. I work with several firms familiar with this process and the other credits outlined in this chapter. This is nothing aggressive that you aren't entitled to, but if you aren't doing it you may be at a competitive disadvantage. If no one has told you this, you might want to ask why?

Not every business owner is eligible for tax credits, but if you are and you aren't picking them up, you may be throwing away tens or even hundreds of thousands of dollars every year.

One of the things I always do with new business clients is make sure they are picking up every legitimate tax credit and deduction they are entitled to. Even if you aren't eligible for tax credits, you probably *are* eligible for the tax exemptions I'm going to introduce in the next chapter.

"Anyone may arrange his affairs so that his taxes shall be as low as possible; he is not bound to choose that pattern which best pays the treasury. There is not even a patriotic duty to increase one's taxes. Over and over again the Courts have said that there is nothing sinister in so arranging affairs as to keep taxes as low as possible. Everyone does it, rich and poor alike and all do right, for nobody owes any public duty to pay more than the law demands."
~Judge Learned Hand

Chapter 11
Additional Exemption Planning for Tax and Asset Protection

In addition to reviewing my client's eligibility for tax credits, I also recommend an exemption analysis for your business. This is a review to see if you are taking all eligible exemptions available to you, for both tax and asset protection purposes.

I obviously cannot do a full exemption analysis of your business in this book, since I don't know anything about it, but I can list the things you might be entitled to. Here are some tax deductions that are also a great way to protect your assets, because many of these tax exemptions are also protected from creditors and lawsuits. I've indicated next to each exemption whether it is also exempt from creditors under federal or state law.

401(k) combined with a Safe Harbor Profit Sharing Plan

These plans are so common I am not going to spend much time on it other than a brief description. A 401(k)-profit-sharing plan is simply a standard 401(k) with an additional profit-sharing option tacked on. The profit-sharing plan accepts something called discretionary employer contributions on behalf of the employee. The IRS limits employer contributions to the profit sharing plan of an employee to 25% of compensation or $53,000, whichever is less. All of your employees must be allowed to participate.

So as an owner you would be able to tax defer and protect (because your money in this plan is absolutely exempt from creditors) up to $53,000 per year. However, if you are a slightly more successful business owner or professional you may wish to take advantage of a significantly larger tax deferral and asset protection plan known as:

Defined Benefit or Qualified Plan

Under section 415(b)(1)(A) the IRS allows you to defer up to $215,000 of your compensation for tax purposes (as of 2017). If you have the income for it, a defined benefit plan could easily have over $2,000,000 of asset protected funds in it over a ten-year period (or significantly more if you get any kind of reasonable return on your investment). The great thing about the defined benefit plan is that everything is absolutely protected from lawsuits and creditors under federal law. Many high income and at-risk professionals like surgeons or physicians in general will often set up a defined benefit plan for these reasons.

The not so great thing about a defined benefit plan is it must be administered by a third-party administrator, and most of them want to manage money in mutual funds inside the plan which limits your investment choices, and therefore your return. Imagine, however, if you could tax defer $215,000 of your income every year and invest in highly appreciating real estate in California, instead of a mutual fund where your advisor tries to tell you 4 % is a good deal.

You should be aware there is no IRS requirement that you can only invest in mutual funds or stocks and bonds. This is a requirement of most investment houses that make money on the sale of their investment offerings, not the IRS. Remember, advisors don't make money on real estate. I work with a TPA who will allow you to have private equity, real estate, and even debt in your plan, so if you able to defer more of your income this is an excellent way to do it. There are legitimate ways to meet the legal requirements of the plan *and* minimize the contribution you must make for other employees. When I tell my "do-it-yourself" clients like contractors and developers that they are allowed to invest in alternative assets, they usually get upset with their existing plan advisor, who told them they must invest in their (heavily fee loaded) mutual fund portfolio. Don't let advisors limit your options and make this plan less attractive than it can be. I can show you how to tax defer while maintaining investment options you would have outside of most defined benefit plans, and it is completely legal and follows the rules.

Non-Qualified Deferred Compensation Plans

Nonqualified deferred compensation plans (NQDC plans) refer to supplemental executive retirement plans (SERPs), voluntary deferral plans, wraparound 401(k) plans, excess benefit plans and equity arrangements, bonus plans and severance pay plans. Under the tax code, if a non-qualified deferred compensation plan meets the requirements of section 409A, the plan benefits are not subject to federal income tax until the compensation is paid to the participant.

So, regardless if you already have or want a defined benefit plan, we can still defer large portions of your taxable income (compensation) and protect it from creditors. Even better, I can show you how to superfund the deferred comp program and give you greater future values leveraging the tax savings. Here's how it works:

The problem with traditional non-qualified plans is the assets are not protected from creditors as they would be in a traditional retirement plan. Additionally, and this is the real problem for most business owners, is that you don't get a current year tax reduction for money put into the plan. The tax deduction is only allowed when the participant takes a distribution from the plan. This is when the company gets the deduction, and when the participant pays taxes on the distribution. What if we could fix that? We'd have to:

- ensure all plan funds, distributions, and death benefits are exempt from creditor attachment and seizure, and
- fund the deferred compensation plan without losing the tax deduction.

Business Succession Planning

Business owners often come to me looking to sell their business. Often there is no third party and they want to sell to company employees or family members (sometimes one in the same). The common situation I hear is this: "I would like to sell to key employees, but they don't have any money. I don't want to sell them the business on an installment note because they have no skin in the game, and I will be sucked back into the business."

All valid points, but with a little bit of planning, and a time horizon as little as three years (depending on sale price, business cash flow, and owner's willingness to exit), we can set aside money that the employees can use as a down payment sufficient to justify a bank loan for the balance. This gives the option of exiting all at once without a promissory note, or with cash and an installment note for some portion if you wish to defer taxes.

By setting up a reasonable vesting schedule on the deferred compensation plan (contributions are deductible to the company when they vest to the employee, whether they take them out or not), and by taking advantage of tax-financed lending, we can use current cash flow to finance an owner's exit, decrease their risk of default on an installment loan, and reduce the business's current tax bill, all while minimizing the owner's tax bill on the sale of the business.

Business succession planning is beyond the scope of this book, but I bring it up because taking advantage of tax exemptions now is one of the best ways to plan for an exit without a reduction in lifestyle. If you don't plan now, you may not like your exit plan or lack thereof.

Captive Insurance

For many years, large corporations in this country have enjoyed benefits from operating their own captive insurance companies. These insurance subsidiaries or affiliates were often domiciled offshore, especially in Bermuda or the Cayman Islands. The risk management benefits of these captives were primary, but their tax advantages were also important. For example, the premium payments are a legitimate business deduction right off the top of your revenue. The premium payment is then placed into a subsidiary "captive" company and invested so there are sufficient funds to pay claims. Typically, the type of insurance offered by the captive is not replacing your property and casualty insurance, but merely supplementing it. Additionally, for small business owners, new captive "pools" have been formed to spread risk even further.

In recent years, smaller, closely held businesses have also learned that the captive insurance entities can provide them significant benefits. These include the attractive risk management elements long appreciated by the larger companies, as well as some nice tax planning opportunities. A properly structured and managed captive insurance company could provide the following tax and non-tax benefits:

- Tax deduction for the parent company for the insurance premium paid to the captive;
- Various other tax savings opportunities, including gift and estate tax savings for the shareholders, and income tax savings for both the captive and the parent;
- Opportunity to accumulate wealth in a tax-favored vehicle;
- Distributions to captive owners at favorable income tax rates (capital gains as opposed to ordinary income;
- Asset protection from the claims of business and personal creditors;
- Reduction in the amount of insurance premiums presently paid by the operating company;
- Access to the lower-cost reinsurance market; and
- Insuring risks that would otherwise be uninsurable.

I will sum it up by giving an example of the tax savings and asset protection available to a business owner or high-income professional who qualifies for a captive.

Let's say the business owner has income of $800,000 per year, and he doesn't need all that income to live on. His captive insurance premium might be $200,000. This $200,000, which would have been taxed as ordinary income, is now a deductible expense invested inside an asset protected captive company unavailable to creditors.

Hence, the investments inside the captive can grow and are protected. If the funds are not used to pay out insurance claims, the owner can take funds out of the captive at capital gains rates when they retire, as opposed to ordinary income. Keep in mind that the captive does pay taxes on its investment income every year, so the money is not tax deferred like a 401(k) or defined benefit plan. However, for those high-income business owners or professionals who would like to reduce and defer taxes until retirement, who would rather take money at the capital gains rates, and who already have a retirement plan, a captive is an attractive option. Of course, a legitimate insurable risk is required in order to be eligible.

Beware that captives set up for tax purposes only, and do not insure a legitimate business risk, can be found to be abusive by the IRS. Overall, captive insurance may be an excellent insurance option, provided that the professionals structuring the arrangements comply with IRS requirements for the formation and maintenance of a captive insurance company.

Ideal candidates for captives are entities that meet the following criteria:

- Profitable business entities seeking substantial annual adjustable tax deductions;
- Businesses with multiple entities or those that can create multiple operating subsidiaries or affiliates;
- Businesses with $500,000 or more in sustainable operating profits;
- Businesses with requisite risk currently uninsured or underinsured;
- Business owner(s) interested in personal wealth accumulation and/or family wealth transfer strategies;
- Businesses where owner(s) are looking for asset protection.

Indeed, captive insurance likely ranks as one of the best business asset protection strategies ever created. It would be very difficult for creditors to prove that payments to a captive for bona fide insurance coverage is fraudulent, since the business received back a substantial economic benefit in insurance coverage from the captive.

Charitable LLC

You've probably heard about Mark Zuckerberg of Facebook and his charitable LLC, but did you know he is still in complete control of the $45 billion worth of stock he and his wife transferred to the LLC? That's right, he can still decide not to give it to charity and take it back if he chooses. How so? It's really very simple and the charitable LLC is nothing new - in fact, it's been around for years. For example, Steve Jobs' widow, Laurene Powell Jobs, created the Emerson Collection, also a charitable LLC, some years prior to the Zuckerberg's more famous entity.

The charitable LLC is more attractive than a foundation or charitable trust due to one big difference: the charitable LLC is not a tax-exempt organization. Therefore, there is no 1023 form filed with the IRS to gain tax-exempt status, because there is no tax exemption. There is no special return, such as a private foundation's 990 PF. The LLC also does not have to meet the 5% annual distribution requirement that applies to charitable foundations. There is no "excess business holdings rule" that limits the percentage of stock that can be held in any one company (hence the Zuckerbergs can have 100% of their Facebook stock holdings), no requirement to follow the "jeopardy investment rule" that precludes investment in speculative start-up companies, no self-dealing rules that limit transactions between founders, and no limitation on expenditures for political purposes.

You may be wondering, with all these advantages, why would anyone set up a charitable foundation (like the Bill and Melinda Gates Foundation, for example)? The answer is that, while the charitable LLC is more flexible, it also does not have the tax advantages of the charitable foundation or trust. The Zuckerbergs received no deduction on income tax when they transferred their Facebook stock to the LLC. On the other hand, Bill Gates received a huge tax deduction which he could take against his ordinary income over a five-year period.

Also, when the Gates foundation sold its Microsoft stock, it paid no capital gains tax, whereas if the Zuckerbergs sell Facebook stock from within the charitable LLC there will be a capital gains tax (although they could avoid it by first donating the stock to charity and letting the charity sell it tax free).

A great thing about the charitable LLC, however, is that by demonstrating your charitable intent by declaring it in the operating agreement, and with a pattern of making at least some charitable donations from the LLC, you are adding a level of asset protection to your holdings that does not exist in a regular non-charitable LLC.

For example, if you remember from Chapter Nine, I pointed out there is only so much of your assets that qualify for a California private retirement plan. In other words, if you are like Mark Zuckerberg, you have way more than you need to live on in retirement. How do you protect the rest? In that case a charitable LLC might be a good option. You can get the assets out of your name, show intent to transfer them to charity, but still maintain control. Plus, if you want, you can actually get some tax benefits along the way.

For example, if Bob Smith from Chapter Eight had more assets than he could exempt, he could use the charitable LLC as an additional level of protection on those excess assets. Here's how it would work:

Let's say Bob has an additional $6 million in real estate. He's not ready to donate it to charity yet, and not sure if he ever wants to. We can set up a charitable LLC and transfer his excess holdings to it. For an extra level of asset protection, I would probably have an independent manager of the LLC, even though Bob and his wife are the only partners. He and his wife would receive all income from the LLC every year as partners on the K-1, except for whatever portion they wanted to donate to charity. Since the LLC is a "pass-through" tax entity, Bob and his wife would receive a charitable deduction on their personal taxes.

An even higher level of asset protection I encourage is to have the charitable LLC set up with voting and non-voting membership interests. Bob and his wife could then make their favorite charity or charities 5% members in the LLC, but Bob and his wife still have all the voting interests. While it is true the charity would be entitled to 5% of the income every year, this transfer of interest gives Bob and his wife an immediate deduction on their income tax of the value of the 5% interest, while they keep control of the assets with 100% of the voting interests. In addition, what do you think the likelihood is of a judge in California dissolving a legitimate charitable LLC, where one of the partners is a charity, and there is history of that partner receiving income from the partnership every year? I would imagine if the interest is large enough the charity would probably pay the legal defense bills to defend the entire LLC from creditors in a lawsuit!

As you can see the charitable LLC is a powerful and flexible planning device, not only for tax savings, but for a higher level of asset protection as well!

Conclusion
Taking Action

"Action is the foundational key to all success".
~ Pablo Picasso

Chapter 12
Next Steps

T hanks for taking the time to read this book. You've taken the time to educate yourself and gone beyond the sound bites. You are a successful entrepreneur or professional who has worked hard, and you don't want anyone taking your assets away, just because we live in a litigious society and an even more litigious state.

You're probably the type of person who doesn't take someone else's word for it. You do the research yourself, and you reach an independent conclusion. If that's the case, then read the summary of cases in the Appendix, as well as the frequently asked questions, before you talk to anyone else about the California private retirement plan. Most (not all) of the advisors I know haven't read these cases, and don't have any knowledge on the subject. Don't take advice on how to protect everything you've worked for your entire life from someone who doesn't have the facts.

If you're like me, you love living in California and you don't want to go to Texas or Florida just to protect a home that you can't leave because it's too hot to go outside anyway.

Take action now. Email me at reed@yesllp.com to schedule a free 20-minute consultation regarding your asset protection plan today. If you don't want to talk to me or if you don't want to wait to see if you qualify, you can use the diagnostic tool at www.trust-cfo.com to quickly see if you are qualified to set up a California Private Retirement Trust[SM]. You can type in my name, Reed Scott, as the referral source. Make sure to scroll to the bottom of the page and hit the submit button, then wait for confirmation of submission before leaving the page. You will get an email back with the summary results. If you qualify, you can contact Trust-CFO™ directly or you can email me for more information.

I hope you found this book useful and practical, because that was my intent. Bookstores are full of literature on asset protection planning, using technical jargon to go over trusts, taxes, and estate planning, but I haven't seen one dedicated to California business owners. I've tried to cut out the legal mumbo jumbo and write in terms that most people understand. I hope it came across that way and does not appear condescending.

I'd love to hear your thoughts, and I'm always open to constructive feedback. If you'd like to drop me a line with your thoughts and comments, please feel free to send them to reed@yesllp.com.

If you're a California resident and you're interested in contacting me about protecting your assets, business or personal, please feel free to email me as well. I'd be happy to walk you through the process of getting started.

Wishing you and your family the best,

Reed Scott

Appendix

Appendix A
RELEVANT PRT CASE LAW SUPPORT SUMMARIES

In re Siegel (134 S. Ct. 1188)

- Summary: Stephen Law filed for protection under Chapter 7 of the United States Bankruptcy Code in 2004. Among the listed assets in the case was *Law's* house in California. *Law* valued his house at approximately $350,000.00 and claimed there were two (2) valid and enforceable mortgages on the property valued at $150,000.00 each (Washington Mutual and Lin's Mortgage & Associates). *Law* asserted his $75,000.00 Homestead Exemption against the property and claimed that the property had no value as a result of same. The Bankruptcy Trustee filed an adversary proceeding against the holder of the second mortgage claiming *Lin's* mortgage was fabricated by the debtor, as *Lin* lived in China and spoke no English. Despite Lin's vigorous defense of his mortgage, the Bankruptcy Court eventually agreed with the Bankruptcy Trustee and surcharged *Law's* exempt interest in the homesteaded property for the hundreds of thousands of dollars in attorney's fees and costs incurred by the Bankruptcy Trustee in pursuit of the action.

- Holding: The courts have no authority under Section 105 of the Bankruptcy Code to surcharge otherwise exempt property for costs incurred by the trustee even when the debtor has engaged in fraudulent actions to protect his interest in the property. Federal law provides no authority for bankruptcy court to deny an exemption on a ground not otherwise specified in the Bankruptcy code.

- Quotes: "But even assuming the Bankruptcy Court could have revisited *Law's* entitlement to the exemption, § 522 does not give courts discretion to grant or withhold exemptions based on whatever considerations they deem appropriate. Rather, the statute exhaustively specifies the criteria that will render property exempt. See § 522(b), (d)."

In re Stern (9th Cir. 2003)

- Summary: Steven Stern filed for bankruptcy after an arbitration award was granted against him. *Stern* than transferred the funds in his IRA to his Profit Sharing Plan the eve before he filed for Chapter 7 Bankruptcy. The Bankruptcy creditors sued *Stern* to set aside the transfer of his IRA into his pension plan as a fraudulent conveyance.
- Holding: Pension Plans are exempt under CCP Section 704.115(b) even though his plan did not qualify under ERISA.
    - Fraud must be evidenced by the preponderance of the evidence. The mere conversion of non-exempt assets to exempt assets is not fraud.
    - No badge of fraud merely because *Stern* lost a multimillion dollar arbitration and filed for bankruptcy --- not enough to meet a preponderance of the evidence.
    - *Grogan, 498 US 111 S. Ct. 654 (1991)* provides that creditors should have the burden to prove that the assets are non-exempt.
    - *In re Love, 341 F.2d 680 (9th Cir. 1965)* provides that conditions surrounding the filing of bankruptcy determines whether the conversion of non-exempt assets to exempt assets is fraudulent.
- Quotes: "We are constrained by our prior opinion in *Wudrick v. Clements,* 451 F.2d 988 (9th Cir.1971). In that case, we ruled "that the purposeful conversion of nonexempt assets to exempt assets on the eve of bankruptcy is not fraudulent per se." *Id.* at 989 (citation omitted).

In re Rucker (9th Cir. 2009)

- Summary: Lloyd Rucker owed more than $6.5 million in civil judgment for four (4) years prior to establishing his Pension Plan and 401(k) Plan. The retirement plans were created by three (3) separate corporations, and the retirement plans were "overfunded." Overfunded means the contributions exceeded the annual limits under IRC, 26 USC Section 401(a)(16).

Further, Rucker funded the retirement plans substantially over what his salaries were from the corporations.

- Holding: After reviewing the totality of the circumstances, there is no state law exemption in an employee retirement plan when the plan was not primarily for retirement purposes and the debtor did not fund the retirement plan correctly.

- Quotes: "A plan used in part to shield assets is still exempt if it was designed and used primarily *for retirement purposes.*" *Dudley*, 249 F.3d at 1176. "We stress that *Rucker* engaged in egregious and deceptive conduct in funding his Plans. He consistently funded his Plans in excess of the contribution limits imposed by the Internal Revenue Code, and he repeatedly and willfully lied to the IRS about the extent of his Plan contributions. *Rucker* also secretly contributed money to his Plans using a wholly owned offshore corporation and a foreign bank account."

In re Cheng (9th Cir. 1991)

- Summary: Ceferino Cheng, MD was the sole shareholder, director, and CEO of the corporation. *Cheng* created two (2) retirement benefit plans for himself.
  - *Cheng* filed for Chapter 7 Bankruptcy and claimed the California Section 704.115 exemption.
  - Bankruptcy Court ruled that the plan were not exempt because *Cheng* was the sole shareholder, director and CEO of the corporation. ☐ "The intent of the legislature in enacting CCP § 704.115 and, in particular, subdivision (e) of that statute, was to impose the "extent necessary" limitation on exempt pension and retirement plan assets when one person who is or is aligned with the debtor has all or substantially all the control over the contributing corporation, the plans, the assets and the determination of the purposes to which they are put. This is the case here, where the debtor was the sole shareholder, president and controlling executive officer of Cheng, M.D., Inc., and also served as the plan's

trustee. Dr. *Cheng* managed and used the plan in a manner that makes it factually more like a self-employed retirement plan or an individual retirement account or annuity than a pension and retirement plan established by a corporation or union in such a fashion that one person does not have control over contributions, management, administration and usage of plan assets. Otherwise stated, the plan operated more like a tax-favored savings account for Dr. *Cheng* than like a negotiated, arms-length pension and retirement system for the benefit of many people."

- Holding: A 'self-employed retirement plan' established by a company, where only one person controls the company and the plan, constitute fully exempted "private retirement plans" under California Section 704.115.
    - o This Court basically argued that the bankruptcy court exceeded its authority to treat a closely held corporation different from a huge corporation. This Court argued that the legislature could have specifically made a distinction between closely-held and large corporations but the legislature did not.
- Quotes "Although the legislative history indicates that the policy behind Section 704.115 (e) is to limit the exemption for plans that are controlled by one person, the statute says what it says, and it was improper for the bankruptcy court to read beyond it. It the California legislature intended to treat closely held corporations differently than large corporations, it could have done so explicitly."

In re Barnes (E.D. California 2002)

- Summary: The Barnes sold their home and purchased an annuity a couple of years before filing bankruptcy; however, the *Barnes* could not produce the annuity contract. *Barnes* owned an annuity and the beneficial interest in two (2) self-settled irrevocable trusts. *Barnes* filed for Chapter 7

- Bankruptcy protection, but the Bankruptcy Trustee filed an action because *Barnes* failed to disclose the annuity. *Barnes* tried to exempt assets of the irrevocable trusts which they cannot do because the assets are the irrevocable trust's assets.
- Holding: A retirement plan must be established by a private employer or employee organization.
  - An annuity contract alone (with no plan) is not deemed a 'private retirement plan'. Under 11 USC Section 521(4), trustee has burden to prove asset is not exempt but debtor failed to produce the annuity contract
- Quotes: *Lieberman,* 245 F.3d at 1094. "No private employer, employee group, or similar organization created the debtors' asserted private retirement plan. The debtors created it. Therefore, the annuity is not a private retirement plan within the meaning of section **704.115**(a)(1)."

In re Crosby

- Summary: Ms. Crosby is the sole shareholder, director and officer of CAT Productions. She is also the sole trustee and beneficiary of the corporation's Profit Sharing plan and Trust Agreement. In 1991, the retirement plan loaned $150,000 to Ms. *Crosby's* aunt and uncle. The aunt and uncle loaned $100,000 and $50,000 to Ms. *Crosby.* Later that year, Ms. *Crosby* withdrew $240,105 from the plan. In 1992, Ms. *Crosby* borrowed an additional $84,000.
- Holding: The private retirement plan was valid because trustee failed to show how the profit-sharing plan was not designed and used for retirement purposes.
- There was no abuse of the retirement plan because Ms. *Crosby* borrowed and repaid a majority of the loan from the retirement plan.
- Quotes "A profit sharing plan constitutes a private retirement plan if it is designed and used for retirement purposes. *C.C.P.* § **704.115**(a)(2). The purpose of this exemption is to safeguard a stream of income for pensioners at the expense of bankruptcy creditors." *In re Witwer,* 148 B.R. at 941.

- o "The court determined that it was inappropriate to examine the plan under a prudent investor test in determining whether it was used for retirement purpose, since even an imprudently invested plan may be designed and used for retirement purposes." *In re Bloom*, 839 F.2d at 1379.
- o "In *In re Bloom,* the Ninth Circuit Court of Appeals held that although the debtor had loaned more than half of the funds in her retirement plan to herself without taking a security interest, her actions did not constitute such an abuse of the plan to cause it to lose its retirement purpose and exemption under California law."
- o "In *Daniels,* the court determined that the debtor abused his retirement plan by using it for current needs since (1) the loans from the plan to the debtor resembled withdrawals; and (2) the debtor utilized the plan to hide otherwise non-exempt assets from creditors. *Id.* at 1357. The Court of Appeals determined that the plan's loan to the debtor were tantamount to a withdrawal for present needs, since the loan amount was substantially equal to the debtor's interest in the plan." In re Daniels, 771 F.2d 1352 (9th Cir. 1985).

In re Cutter (9th Cir. 2008)

- Summary: Edward Williams Cutter II created a self-settled trust where the beneficiary were his unnamed descendants. The Trust provided for the vesting upon settlor's death and the trustor/trustee retained the power to deplete the trust corpus for the benefit of the settlor.
- Holding: The trust corpus was included in the Bankruptcy estate because the trust was self-settled (debtor had a beneficial and equitable interest in the Trust) and the debtor had the power to act for the Trust for his benefit.
- Quotes: "In summary, to the extent Debtor was the trustee of the Trust, he possessed the power (at his sole discretion) to invade the corpus and make distributions from the Trust for his

own benefit. The entire corpus…is therefore property of the (bankruptcy) estate."

In re McKown (9th Cir. 1999)

- Summary: Mr. and Mrs. McKown filed for Chapter 7 Bankruptcy and claimed their IRA as exempt. The IRA was worth $6,413.14.
- Holding: An IRA qualifies for exemption under Federal and California language.
- Quotes: "The Fifth Circuit held, in *Carmichael v. Osherow,* that an IRA is a "similar plan or contract" under the federal statute. The Second Circuit held in *Dubroff v. First National Bank,* that, under New York language materially identical to the federal and California statutory language, an IRA is exempt as a "similar plan or contract."

In re Metz (9th Cir. 1998)

- Summary: Gail E. Metz formed Gail Mills Construction Co., Inc. where she was the managing officer and held a contractor's license back in 1980. In 1981, *Metz* was no longer an employee but was involved in the management of the corporation. In 1981, the corporation created a Defined Benefit Plan for *Metz's* husband. Subsequently, the *Metz* divorce and Gail was awarded an undivided one-half interest in the community property.
- Holding: When a plan participant has no control or dominion over the plan, the spendthrift provision remains valid. Therefore, the plan will fall outside the bankruptcy estate.
- Quotes: "Under 11 U.S.C. § 541(c)(2), property is excluded from the estate if it contains an anti-alienation provision enforceable under state law." *In re Moses,* 215 B.R. 27, 35 (9th Cir. BAP 1997).
  - "The court noted that the debtor had taken no loans or disbursements, the debtor did not contribute more than he was entitled, and he had no part in administering the plan" *Schwartzman,* 57 Cal.Rptr.2d at 797. "The court opined that the 'kind of control' which would show a

non-retirement purpose would be substantially all control over contributions, management, administration, and use of fund, and there is no such evidence here."

o "An individual retirement account (IRA) is similar to a pension and profit sharing plan. *In re Chiz,* 142 B.R. 592, 592–93 (Bankr.D.Mass.1992). In *Rawlinson v. Kendall, (In re Rawlinson),* 209 B.R. 501 (9th Cir. BAP 1997), the court held that an IRA was exempt even though the debtor could withdraw funds at will. The court stated that the rule of *ejusdem generis* requires inclusion of IRAs as exemptions within the meaning of Cal.Civ.Proc.Code § 703.140(b)(10)(E)." *Rawlinson,* 209 B.R. at 507.

o "In *In re McKown,* 203 B.R. 722 (Bankr.E.D.Cal.1996), the court held that IRAs come within the scope of Cal.Civ.Proc.Code § 703.140(b)(10)(E) because they are 'aimed to enable working taxpayers to accumulate assets during their productive years so that they might draw upon them during retirement.'" *McKown,* 203 B.R. at 724 (quoting *In re Bates,* 176 B.R. 104, 107 (Bankr.D.Me.1994)). "The court said, '[w]hile it is true a debtor can withdraw funds deposited into an IRA, premature withdrawal... carries a penalty.'" *McKown,* 203 B.R.at 725.

o "The Debtor did not administer the Plan and did not make withdrawals, or borrow from the Plan after her dissolution. Presumably she could not terminate the Plan without her former spouse's and the State court's consent, which retained jurisdiction. The ability to make a withdrawal, without more, is not sufficient to destroy its spendthrift character." *John Hancock Mut. Life Ins. Co. v. Watson (In re Kincaid),* 917 F.2d 1162, 1168 (9th Cir.1990). "Accordingly, the Debtor's degree of control is not so great as to void the anti-alienation provision of the Plan and make it non-enforceable under state spendthrift trust law."

    o   "The Ninth Circuit held that the debtor's interest in the assets accumulated during her relationship with her domestic partner was not an interest in a retirement plan because it was not an interest in a right to future payments in recognition of her employment. It was a judgment in a fixed amount to be paid in $3,000 installments." *Wilbur,* 126 F.3d at 1220.

In re Mooney

- Summary: Mr. *Mooney* worked at Southern California Edison where his employer set up an Edison Retirement Plan, which was ERISA-qualified. Mr. *Mooney* rolled his ERISA funds into his IRAs. One IRA he took a payment stream and the other he withheld until the age of 65.
- Holding: Funds rolled over from ERISA qualified plans into IRAs were exempt under California law only to the extent necessary for retirement.
- Quotes "This is because the CCP § **704.115** exemption statute separates out private retirement plans from IRAs and annuities. *See* CCP § **704.115**(a)(1)-(3). Under this statutory scheme, the California legislature provided a full exemption for private retirement plans, but not for IRAs and annuities."

In re Moses (9th Cir. 1999)

- Summary: Mr. and Mrs. Moses filed for Chapter 7 Bankruptcy and claimed their Keogh Plan established by the Southern California Permanente Medical Group Retirement Plan as exempt from the bankruptcy estate. The retirement plan is a profit-sharing plan where benefits were payable only upon a participant's termination, retirement, disability or death.
- Holding: A self-employed retirement plan with spendthrift provisions fall under California exemption statute if the trust was not self-settled, the plan was administered by a third party, plan participant could not terminate or amend the retirement plan, and plan participant had no access to plan until death, disability, or retirement.

- Quotes "In this case, the BAP properly concluded that the anti-alienation provision in the Keogh Plan sufficiently divorced the Debtors from control over the trust corpus. First, the trust was not self-settled because SCPMG, not the Debtors, was the settlor of the trust. Second, SCPMG created and administered the Plan. Third, Debtors did not have the ability to terminate or amend the Plan. Once Debtor *Moses* decided to join the plan, that decision was irrevocable. Finally, Debtors did not have access to the Plan until Debtor Moses' retirement."
  - "Ehrenberg's surplusage argument fails, however, for the same reasons that the petitioner's argument failed in *Patterson.* First, § **704.115** exempts from the bankruptcy estate a much broader category of interests than spendthrift law excludes."
  - "We should respect this principle of California jurisprudence. Moreover, not to respect it would ignore the structure of **704.115**. The section's placement indicates an intent on the part of the legislature to draft an *exemption,* not an *exclusion,* for self-employed retirement plans such as Debtors' Keogh Plan."
  - "Third, § **704.115** is not rendered inoperative by our decision. It applies in situations other than bankruptcy proceedings. It applies to all situations where a judgment creditor seeks money from a judgment debtor. The statute prevents the creditor from reaching the entire corpus of a trust-it allows the debtor to maintain the corpus to the extent necessary for the debtor's support." *See, e.g., Yaesu Elecs. Corp. v. Tamura,* 28 Cal.App.4th 8, 33 Cal.Rptr.2d 283 (Cal.Ct.App.1994).

In re Phillips (206 B.R. 196 1997)

- Summary: Mr. and Mrs. *Phillips* filed for Chapter 13 Bankruptcy and claims their private retirement plan and private retirement trust as exempt under California law. The *Phillips* established their **informal** retirement plan in 1977. There was nothing evidenced in writing the *Phillips* used the purported assets of the trust for various purposes but none related to retirement. In 1985, the *Phillips* executed a revocable trust that was created for probate avoidance. The trust was never used for retirement purposes. None of the assets identified in Schedule A showed the house but the house was never funded into the trust. Further, a mutual fund account held in the Trust was denominated "non-retirement" account.

- o The *Phillips* were the participants, sponsors, administrators and trustees of the retirement plan. Other plans had third parties to serve in a role and other plans had assets that were funded outside of the participants' assets.
- o The *Phillips* funded their house into the Trust but the house was not a revenue or income producing asset.

- Holding: Self-settled trusts fall outside California Civil Code of Procedures Section 704.115.
  - o Informal retirement plans are not considered private retirement plan.
- Quotes "The California Legislature confirmed the rule of *Nelson* in California Probate Code section 15304(a) which states, in part: If the settlor is a beneficiary of a trust created by the settlor and the settlor's interest is subject to a provision restraining the voluntary or involuntary transfer of the settlor's interest, the restraint is invalid against transferees or creditors of the settlor."
  - o "Debtors also rely on numerous cases involving individuals who enjoy the benefits of section 704.115(a) via their own private retirement plans. But those cases all involve third parties, even though in some cases those third parties are wholly-controlled professional corporations of the debtors."
  - o "Debtors also rely on numerous cases involving individuals who enjoy the benefits of section 704.115(a) via their own private retirement plans. But those cases all involve third parties even though in some cases those third parties are wholly-controlled professional

corporations of the debtors. *In re Bloom, supra,* involved a corporate retirement plan created eight years prior to bankruptcy. The debtor was one of two owners of the medical corporation that created the plan. In *In re MacIntyre, supra,* the debtors were two married physicians employed by a non-profit hospital that withheld from their paychecks contributions to an Internal Revenue Code § 403b retirement annuity. *In re Witwer,* 148 B.R. 930, 939 (Bankr.C.D.Cal.1992), concerned the debtor's own medical professional corporation as did *In re Cheng,* 943 F.2d 1114, 1116 (9th Cir.1991). In *In re Crosby,* 162 B.R. 276 (Bankr.C.D.Cal.1993), the debtor claimed exempt her interest in a profit sharing plan established by her wholly-owned corporation, CAT Productions."

- o "The Retirement Plan resembles in name only a private retirement plan intended for such purposes; names alone are not controlling." *Bloom,* 839 F.2d at 1378.

In re Reid (139 B.R. 19 1992)

- Summary: Larry Reid was employed by General Dynamics Corporation, and the corporation created a Savings & Stock Investment Plan (ERISA plan). The plan contains an anti-alienation and anti-assignment provision. The corporation is the plan administrator and named beneficiary, and the corporation manages and controls the plan. *Reid* can only access the trust corpus upon retirement, death, disability or termination of employment. The plan permitted loans and hardships so the employee can access funds. *Reid* self-terminated his employment and did NOT request any distribution.
  - o *Reid* filed for Chapter 7 Bankruptcy and claimed the plan was exempt like an IRA.
  - o Debtor had control of the plan because had can demand distribution and can manipulate the control of his distribution.

- Holding: A debtor who can exercise control over his trust does not constitute a California spendthrift trust.
- Quotes "At the date of filing bankruptcy, the debtor was no longer an employee of the Corporation. Tus, under the terms of the Plan, the debtor has the right to demand a lump sum distribution at any time. This right allows the debtor to manipulate the trust for his own purposes and control the timing of his distributions. Because the debtor has unrestricted access to the funds, the court concludes that the debtor's Plan does not constitute a valid spendthrift trust. Thus, the Plan is not excludable from the debtor's estate."

In re Vigghiany (74 B.R. 61 1987)

- Summary: Robert G. Vigghiany was a self-employed electrical contractor who established IRAs for himself. *Vigghiany* filed for Chapter 7 Bankruptcy and claimed his two (2) IRAs were exempt from creditors under California Code of Civil Procedure Section 704.115.
- Holding: Debtor's IRAs were exempt under California Code of Civil Procedure Section 704.115.
- Quotes "In enacting C.C.P. § 703.130, California effectively opted out of the federal exemption scheme. However, simultaneously, the California legislature enacted C.C.P. § 703.140. This section allows debtors to choose either the exemptions that state law already provided for or to choose the exemptions contained therein."
  - "IRA's are included within the meaning of "private retirement plans" in C.C.P. § **704.115**... Under C.C.P. § **704.115**, whether or not the debtor has control over the account is irrelevant to the exemption...However, the amount of the exemption can be challenged and pursuant to C.C.P. § **704.115**(e) the exemption is limited to the amount necessary to provide for the support of the judgment debtor upon retirement and for the support of the spouse and dependents of the judgment debtor."

Schwartzman v. Wilshinsky (50 Cal. App. 4th 619)

- Summary: A judgment was granted in favor of Blake Schwartzman for $1.75 million against Stephen Wilshinsky. *Wilshinsky* filed a claim of exemption on his IRA and 401(k) pursuant to California 704.115.
    - o The IRA was established by *Wilshinsky* former employer before he transferred it to Sutro & Co.
    - o Sutro & Co. created the 401(k) Plan and Trust Agreement for *Wilshinsky*. 401(k) Plan is administered by an Administrative Committee, 3 trustees were nominated, no ability to withdraw until 59 1/2 unless financial hardship, and no ability to manage the plan or disregard the plan rules.
- Holding: IRA is only protected to the necessity of debtor or debtor's dependents.
    - o Funds in private retirement plan established by Debtor's employer were exempt regardless of whether funds were contributed by the employer or debtor-employee.
- Quotes: "If property is claimed as exempt pursuant to a provision exempting property to the extent necessary for the support of the judgment debtor and the spouse and dependents of the judgment debtor, the claim of exemption shall include a financial statement (Code Civ.Proc., § 703.530, subd. (a))."
    - o "In contrast, another bankruptcy debtor took loans from her retirement account, but she followed the procedures set out in the plan, signed promissory notes, and paid reasonable interest; and there was no indication that she used the account to hide ineligible assets. (See e.g. *In re Bloom* (9th Cir.1988) 839 F.2d 1376, 1379.) The court held that the loans were not so abusive as to indicate a non-retirement purpose." (*Ibid.*)
    - o "The kind of control which would show a non-retirement purpose would be substantially all control over contributions, management, administration, and use of funds, and there is no such evidence here. (See *In re Cheng* (9th Cir.1991) 943 F.2d 1114, 1116.)"

Wudrick v. Clements (9th Cir. 1971)

- Summary: Mr. and Mrs. Roon was advised by their bankruptcy counsel to enhance their exemptions. The *Roons* got a bank loan and paid off their car and deposited $800 in their Savings & Loan Association. Three weeks later, the *Roons* filed for bankruptcy.
- Holding: No fraud can be proved by the deliberate conversion of nonexempt assets to exempt assets.
- Quotes "…the purposeful conversion of exempt assets on the eve of bankruptcy is not fraudulent per se. *In re Dudley*, 72 F. Supp. 942, 945-947 (D.Cal. 1947), aff'd per curiam, *Goggin v. Dudley*, 155 F.2d 1023 (9th Cir. 1948); *Love v. Menick*, 341 F.2d 680, 682-683 (9th Cir. 1965)"
  - "The Court of Appeals held that conversion of non-exempt assets to exempt assets on the eve of bankruptcy by creation of secured debts and deposit of the proceeds in exempt accounts, in each case by securing loan on motor vehicle and placing part of the proceeds in either an exempt savings and loans account or exempt shares in credit union were not fraudulent as a matter of law, and claims of exemption based on such transfers were valid." (11 U.S.C. Section 24)."

McMullen v. Haycock

- Summary: McMullen sued Don Haycock for malicious prosecution. McMullen was granted a $515,000 judgment against *Haycock*. *Haycock* transferred funds from his private retirement plan, established by Hughes Aircraft Company into an IRA.
  - Haycock argued that pursuant to California Section 703.080(a), the assets can be traced from the fully exempt private retirement plan so the IRA should remain fully exempt.

- Holding: An IRA is not subject to the "extent necessary for support" limitation when the IRA is funded and traced to a private retirement plan.
- Quotes "Section 703.080 states that "[s]ubject to any limitation provided in the particular exemption, a fund that is exempt remains exempt to the extent that it can be traced into deposit accounts or in the form of cash or its equivalent" (§ 703.080, subd. (a))."
  - "*In re Mooney* (Bankr.C.D.Cal.2000) 248 B.R. 391, in which a federal bankruptcy court held, in a case of first impression, that the debtors' exempt funds from a private retirement account were no longer fully exempt after they were rolled over into an IRA."
  - "In the absence of statutory limitations on the tracing of funds distributed from private retirement plans, we can think of no reason not to trace fully exempt private retirement plan funds under section 703.080, subdivision (a) to their new location or account and continue to apply the full exemption, regardless of the type of exemption that would otherwise apply to the new account without the tracing statute."
  - "The exemption statutes should be construed, so far as practicable, to the benefit of the judgment debtor." (*Schwartzman v. Wilshinsky, supra,* 50 Cal.App.4th at p. 630, 57 Cal.Rptr.2d 790.)

Appendix B
California Private Retirement Trust^{SM}
FAQ for Clients*

This appendix is provided courtesy of Trust-CFO™, a third-party administrator experienced in set up and administration of California private retirement plans. The author is an independent attorney and is not an employee of Trust-CFO™. You are not required to use this TPA as an administrator for your California private retirement plan.

• *What is the California Private Retirement Trust^{SM} (PRT^{SM})?*

The PRT^{SM} is a proprietary trust designed to specifically support a private retirement plan as regulated under California exemption law, statute Code of Civil Procedure 704.115(b), in which all plan funds (assets), distributions and death benefits are exempt from creditor attachment and seizure.

• *What is so unique about the PRT^{SM}?*

The PRT^{SM} is the only trust design that allows for the funding of private assets on a participant's private balance sheet (old monies) in order to make up the substantial savings shortfall and related income gap at retirement.

All other private retirement plans are limited to contributions (funding) from the employer out of participant earnings and/or through employer profits (considered new monies).

• *What type of trust is a PRT^{SM}?*

A PRT^{SM} is a non-qualified irrevocable employee grantor trust, and is tax-neutral. It is not a aualified plan or IRA, which are regulated under ERISA and federal bankruptcy laws.

• *Am I giving away my assets to others, like an irrevocable estate trust?*

No, the PRT^{SM} is a non-gifting trust. You are simply contributing assets to your own retirement trust and you retain beneficial interests to plan funds during your lifetime. As such, it does not remove the plan assets from your estate and therefore does not reduce estate taxes.

• *What if something happens to me?*

You designate a contingent and remote beneficiary in your plan document. If the PRT^{SM} is properly administrated, your beneficiaries can continue to receive exemption protection on survivor benefits during their lifetime.

• *Can I establish my own PRT^{SM}?*

No, a PRT^{SM} cannot be self-settled in California. A business must be the settlor of the PRT^{SM}.

• *What assets can I put in my PRT^{SM}?*

Any appreciating assets that have been properly identified and can be considered legitimate for retirement are reasonable to contribute.

• *What assets can I not put in my PRT^{SM}?*

Your personal residence, any depreciating or personal use assets, or assets *not* proper for retirement.

• *Are there any contribution limits to funding my PRT^{SM}?*

No, there are no limits to funding amounts, but there must be a "means-testing" analysis done to prove a legitimate need for additional private retirement funding.

• Can I just simply transfer assets to my PRT^{SM}?

No, to qualify for exemption status, PRT^{SM} assets must first be properly recharacterized from "non-exempt" to "exempt". *This is a critical process and should only be handled by TRUST-CFO^{TM}.*

• Do I get a tax deduction for my contributions?

No, the California PRT^{SM} intentionally does not seek tax deductions for contributions, because it supports the pass-through of expenses, deductions and tax credits already received by "active" assets funded into the plan. A tax deduction would weaken the assets protected in the trust.

Note TRUST-CFO^{TM} offers a Qualified PRT^{SM} plan design that allows clients to fund deductible contributions against earnings, and still allocate those funds to private investments, but is regulated by ERISA limitations.

• How are my PRT^{SM} assets taxed?

The PRT^{SM} is tax-neutral so assets are taxed as if owned by the grantor/participant. Because there is no change in basis, the grantor/participant avoids negative tax triggers on income, capital gain or property taxes.

• Do I need to do some additional reporting?

Yes, the PRT^{SM} requires a 1041 Trust Tax Return to formally identify assets owned by the trust, which is used to strengthen creditor exemption defense. However, the income and gains are reported on the grantor's personal tax returns, as if owned directly.

• Do I get any other tax benefits?

Yes, with proper administration you can retain the tax benefits associated with any active assets, including business expenses. *This is a critical process and should only be handled by TRUST-CFO^{TM}.*

• *Can I manage and self-direct my own assets?*

Yes, while the PRT^SM requires an independent trustee to secure exemption protection benefits, you can still make decisions and oversee your own PRT^SM private asset, business, and investment strategy.

• *Are there any limits or rules to my funding strategy?*

No, there are no "prudent-man" rules or "prohibited transactions" like with qualified retirement plans and self-directed individual retirement accounts (IRAs). You can fund, and therefore protect, any commercial or private investments, including your private business stock/partnership or membership interests. You can even fund promissory notes and make trust loans, as well as sign as indemnitor for commercial loans, bonding or surety collateralization needs.

• *Are there any participation requirements for my PRT^SM?*

No, you can select whomever you want to participate in a plan, and each participant has his or her own PRT^SM to receive customized plan benefits.

• *Can I participate in both a qualified plan and my PRT^SM?*

Yes, as a matter of fact a qualified retirement plan (QRP) and a PRT^SM complement each other and should be integrated to ensure maximum creditor exemptions and tax exemptions, including tax-deductions for contributions.

• *Does my PRT^SM provide any benefits other than retirement?*

Yes, a PRT^SM can provide solutions and benefits for a multitude of retirement needs, including executive compensation planning for business needs and survivor retirement planning for personal needs. * *Please consult with a pre-approved and licensed PRT^SM law firm.*

• *When can I take distributions?*

You can start plan distributions as soon as day 1, year 2 after initial funding of your PRT™, if as planned and scheduled in the plan design. There are no 59 ½ (10%) or 70 ½ (50%) RMD penalties for a California PRT^{SM} like those imposed under qualified (ERISA) plans.

• *Do I have to take distributions?*

Yes, if scheduled, then the PRT^{SM} must make mandatory plan distributions to satisfy the Plan agreement and assure plan legitimacy.

• *Are my distributions exposed to creditors?*

No, under 704.115 all plan distributions, as well as death benefits, maintain exemption from creditor attachment, as long as they are not commingled (tainted) with other exposed assets/accounts. * *This is a critical admin process and should only be handled by TRUST-CFO™.*

• *What if my PRT^{SM} asset values grow more than planned?*

The trustee allows for discretionary distributions on excess growth or gains above mandatory distributions, which maintain ongoing exemption protection if properly administrated.

• *Do I lose my creditor exemption protection of my PRT^{SM} funds and benefits if distributed from my plan?*

No, if distributions are made to a pre-designated PRT^{SM} Distribution Account, then funds can continue to receive ongoing asset-protection from creditor attachment/judgment. However, this must be properly administrated so as not to forfeit benefits.

• *Are there any penalties for early or late distributions?*

No, there are no pre-59 ½ (10% penalty) or post-70 ½ (50% penalty) excise tax penalties.

• *Can I take a loan from my PRT^{SM}?*

Yes, PRT^{SM} loans are fully permitted and supported by case law, and can be a powerful business cash flow management technique as well as add an additional layer of equity and earnings protection, if properly administrated.

• *What are the parameters for PRT^{SM} loans?*

There is no maximum loan from a PRT^{SM}, as long as it is arm's length. Loans above $50,000 must be secured with friendly liens on outside collateral. These secured loans offer extremely flexible terms at fair market value applicable federal rates.

• *How much is the PRT^{SM} cost to set up?*

Setup costs include a Plan Setup fee typically ranging from $2,500 to $7,500, with average of $4,500. Note that Plan setup costs are a deductible expense to the sponsoring business, so your net cost to Plan asset values is extremely low, usually $1/10^{th}$ of the cost-benefit of a qualified plan (401(k)) cost.

• *What are the annual management costs for a PRT^{SM}?*

The PRT^{SM} annual administration depends on the intensity of asset reporting. Annual administration fees range from $2,500 to $15,000. Administration costs/fees are paid and expensed out of PRT^{SM} account corpus quarterly.

• *Are there any additional costs or fees associated with my PRT^{SM} Plan assets?*

No, pricing is flat-fee based and not asset under management (AUM) based, as with other invasive commercial trust companies. This ensures a high benefit-cost ratio that improves substantially in value over time.

• *What if the state law changes?*

There are no guarantees, however, the legislation statute that regulates the state exemption code has been in existence and remains unchanged since 1970, and pre-dating ERISA qualified plans (401k), so it is the foundation for all other retirement planning as well as is the basis of California exemption law.

• *What are my next steps to find out if the PRT^{SM} is right for me?*

Get a free PRT^{SM} Diagnostic & PRT^{SM} Plan Proposal: go to http://trust-cfo.com/exemption-planning/exemption-diagnostic-calculator/ to assess if you qualify, and get immediate answers.

Made in the USA
Columbia, SC
29 December 2017